Young Carers and their Families

36278EC. £13·99

Other titles in the series

Introduction to Therapeutic Play
J. Carroll
0-632-04148-X

Patterns of Adoption
D. Howe
0-632-04149-8

Family Group Conferences in Child Welfare
P. Marsh and G. Crow
0-632-04922-7

Neglected Children: issues and dilemmas
O. Stevenson
0-632-04146-3

Child Welfare in the UK
Edited by O. Stevenson
0-632-04993-6

Also available from Blackwell Science

Child and Family Social Work
Editor: Professor David Howe
ISSN 1356-7500

Child and Family Social Work is a major international journal for all those concerned with the social and personal well-being of children and those who care for them. The Journal publishes original and distinguished contributions on matters of research, theory, policy and practice in the field of social work with children and their families. It aims to give international definition to the discipline and practice of child and family social work.

Child and Family Social Work is published quarterly

WORKING TOGETHER FOR CHILDREN,
YOUNG PEOPLE AND THEIR FAMILIES

SERIES EDITOR: PROFESSOR OLIVE STEVENSON

Young Carers and their Families

Saul Becker
Jo Aldridge
Chris Dearden

Blackwell
Science

© 1998 by
Blackwell Science Ltd
Editorial Offices:
Osney Mead, Oxford OX2 0EL
25 John Street, London WC1N 2BL
23 Ainslie Place, Edinburgh EH3 6AJ
350 Main Street, Malden
    MA 02148 5018, USA
54 University Street, Carlton
    Victoria 3053, Australia
10, rue Casimir Delavigne
    75006 Paris, France

Other Editorial Offices:

Blackwell Wissenschafts-Verlag GmbH
Kurfürstendamm 57
10707 Berlin, Germany

Blackwell Science KK
MG Kodenmacho Building
7–10 Kodenmacho Nihombashi
Chuo-ku, Tokyo 104, Japan

First published 1998

Set in 10/12 pt Sabon
by DP Photosetting, Aylesbury, Bucks
Printed and bound in Great Britain by
MPG Books Ltd, Bodmin, Cornwall

DISTRIBUTORS

Marston Book Services Ltd
PO Box 269
Abingdon
Oxon OX14 4YN
(*Orders:* Tel: 01235 465500
              Fax: 01235 465555)

USA
Blackwell Science, Inc.
Commerce Place
350 Main Street
Malden, MA 02148 5018
(*Orders:* Tel: 800 759 6102
              781 388 8250
        Fax: 781 388 8255)

Canada
Login Brothers Book Company
324 Saulteaux Crescent
Winnipeg, Manitoba R3J 3T2
(*Orders:* Tel: 204 224-4068)

Australia
Blackwell Science Pty Ltd
54 University Street
Carlton, Victoria 3053
(*Orders:* Tel: 03 9347 0300
        Fax: 03 9347 5001)

A catalogue record for this title
is available from the British Library

ISBN 0-632-04966-9

Contents

Foreword
by Professor Olive Stevenson

I am very pleased to have this book in the series. We are indebted to Saul Becker, Jo Aldridge and Chris Dearden for the work which they have done in raising awareness, nationally and internationally, of the difficult and sensitive issues concerning young carers in society. This book marks another step along the way. It is a comprehensive discussion of complex problems. It considers the role of children and young people in looking after other people, often adults; the tension between different views about and concepts of disability; the legal and policy implications of the children's position; and the challenge for service providers.

The authors discuss the concerns which have been expressed by those who represent the views of the social movement for disabled people. This group argues that an emphasis on the needs and problems of young carers may further emphasise the limitations of disabled parents, rather than their rights and needs for comprehensive support services within a society which adapts itself to their requirements. If the needs of the adults were met, 'young carers' as a category would disappear.

It is indeed the case that 'the career' of an idea or of a policy initiative can lead to unintended consequences or distortions of the original. There are such dangers in 'the career' of this idea; Becker, Aldridge and Dearden have quite literally put the issue of young carers 'on the map'.

But I believe that their work can and should benefit the families as a whole, when some of its members are disabled. As is argued in this book, an approach to the issue which can lead to the assessment of young carers as 'children in need', under the provisions of the Children Act 1989, can provide much needed support to the family generally as well as to particular children. It should mesh with services provided under the Community Care legislation.

There are pragmatic reasons for following this course as well as more fundamental justifications. The pragmatic reasons are twofold. Whatever disabled people rightly claim for their social inclusion in the long term, it is abundantly clear that we are many years away from achieving it. For most disabled people and for workers in the field, it is a matter of getting what you can, when you can. We have a moral obligation to give some children back their childhood, before it is too late. The present debate on the 'refocusing' of children's services offers a good opportunity to include young carers in strategies and planning for children and families generally, and for all those who require particular support. Thus, we may be able to avoid separating young carers from their peers whilst, of course, recognising that they have certain unique requirements. It goes without saying (but at present is easier said than done) that a vital element in young carers' support is the support offered to the disabled relatives themselves, but there are also distinctive needs which the young carer him or herself may have, such as for some fun and relaxation.

Another reason for following the 'children in need' route is that it may go some way to alleviating the widespread fear that to come to the notice of the authorities may lead to children being removed from home. Young carers and their parents 'caught' this fear, which arises not from the evidence of actual practice but from public and professional anxiety about abuse.

There are also two more fundamental justifications for focusing the searchlight on young carers. First, we have an abundance of well established research on the prerequisites for 'good enough' development in childhood. These have been crystallised in a raft of work supported by the Department of Health on the assessment of the well-being of 'Looked after Children' and are now being applied to children in their own families. I have suggested elsewhere that this work has particular applicability to the assessment of 'neglected' children for whom a holistic approach is essential. Similar considerations apply to young carers; this is not to suggest that their circumstances are necessarily similar to neglected children but that the 'seven dimensions' identified by these materials, such as 'identity' and education, give us a proper yardstick for planning the support which such children may need for their development. As this book indicates, however, careful research will be needed to examine further the precise effects on the development of young carers of assuming certain adult roles.

Finally, this book should encourage us to a more sophisticated understanding of the dynamic interplay between carer and cared for. We will never provide support which is sensitively tuned to need unless we recognise that dependency is a complex and shifting phenomenon. Whether or not the dependency of an adult on a child is destructive to the child goes far beyond what a child actually does for an adult, to the underlying relationship between them. The effects on children of being powerless and yet powerful remain to be further probed.

I am confident that this book will encourage further debate in a crucially important field.

Olive Stevenson
Professor Emeritus of Social Work Studies
University of Nottingham

Acknowledgements

We are grateful to the many individuals and organisations who, over the last five years, have helped us develop our research and thinking on young carers and their families. In particular, we would like to thank the Calouste Gulbenkian Foundation, and especially the Director of the UK Branch, Ben Whitaker, for all his support and encouragement. It would be fair to say that without the Foundation's financial support the Young Carers Research Group could never have been formed and awareness of young carers' issues would be far more limited.

We are also grateful to Nottingham Health Authority, Crossroads, and the Carers National Association for the financial support they have given. Again, this support has been vital in enabling us to develop the work of the Young Carers Research Group.

We would like to thank Jon North, co-ordinator of the Nottinghamshire Association of Voluntary Organisations, for introducing us to the issue of young carers in the first place, and to members of the Nottinghamshire Young Carers Steering Group.

Others have been instrumental in developing our thinking, in particular Francine Bates, Sylvia Heal, Huw Meredith and Jill Pitkeathley.

We would also like to thank the many young carers project workers and young carers themselves who have patiently provided us with information and agreed to be interviewed by us for a number of research studies, many of which are reported in this volume. Without their support, much of our work would have been impossible.

Our thanks to Olive Stevenson for inviting us to write this book as part of the series 'Working Together for Young People and their Families', and to Sarah-Kate Powell and Griselda Campbell at Blackwell Science for their assistance.

Loughborough University has been an excellent home for the Young Carers Research Group, in both encouraging us to develop and expand our programme of work and being flexible and supportive. Our thanks especially to Jochen Clasen, David Deacon, Peter Golding, Arthur Gould, Linda Hantrais, Steve Hughes and Ruth Lister.

We would also like to thank Dave Everitt of Eco Consulting and Betty Newton, another member of the Young Carers Research Group, who has helped in a number of projects and has provided the efficient administration for the Group, dealing with orders for publications and requests for information from the UK and abroad and freeing time for us to get on with this book.

For their patience and understanding during the writing of this book, we would like to thank our families, especially Kay and Brian Aldridge for all their help with child care!

To Fiona (SB), David, Jack and Luke (JA) and Marc (CD)

Introduction

Themes and concerns

Young carers are children and young people under the age of 18 who provide care to another family member, usually a parent, who has a physical illness or disability, mental ill-health, a sensory disability, is misusing drugs or alcohol, or who is frail. Many of these young carers will experience restrictions on their childhood development or in their transition to adulthood. For example, their education may suffer because they find it difficult to attend school on a regular basis or to concentrate while at school, or they may find it difficult to make time and space for leisure activities or recreation with their peers. Some may experience physical injury as a consequence of lifting parents, while others may experience emotional harm related to the degree of responsibility they have in caring *for* and caring *about* an ill or disabled family member.

While some degree of caring in childhood is both routine and to be valued and encouraged as a part of a 'healthy' child's development, young carers are children who are involved in exaggerated levels or types of caring, which often impact negatively on them. For example, some young carers may be providing care for many hours per day; others may be providing less care in terms of hours, but the care may be of an intimate (for example toileting, bathing) or physically injurious nature (for example lifting and carrying). The 'official' Department of Health definition refers to young carers as children who are providing, or are intending to provide, a 'substantial amount of care on a regular basis'. The Department also acknowledges that some young carers may not provide substantial or regular care but that their development may nonetheless be impaired as a result of their caring responsibilities (Department of Health, 1996a, b). These issues are discussed in some depth in Chapters 1 and 2 of this volume. Despite no universally accepted definition as to what precisely constitutes a 'young carer', there is now considerable agreement regarding the characteristics that define the experiences and condition of young carers, namely their involvement in levels or forms of caring which have a restrictive or negative impact on their childhood.

In the UK, almost three million children under the age of 16 (equivalent to 23% of all children) live in households where one family member is 'hampered in daily activities by any chronic physical or mental health problem, illness or disability' (Eurostat, 1997). In Europe as a whole, nearly a quarter of all children (16 million in total) live in households of this type. In the United States, data show that while 75% of 'informal' carers are female, almost one third of these women have children at home who are under 12 years of age, and 23% have a child aged between 12 and 17 living with them (Beach, 1997). It is impossible to estimate what proportion of these European (including British) and American children do or do not take on caring responsibilities within the family. However, official figures for Britain indicate that approximately 50 000 children can be termed 'young carers'. Other researchers, however, have suggested that the real figure may be significantly higher (Aldridge & Becker, 1993a; Dearden & Becker, 1995a). These data and issues are explored in some detail in Chapters 1 and 2, while cross-national data are presented in Chapter 4.

The argument that *caring* itself can have a negative impact or restrict children's development has been challenged by some authors associated with the disability movement. As we show in Chapters 1 and 3, these authors have attacked the use of the term 'young carer' and have argued that it is not caring *per se* which restricts children's lives, but rather the failure of welfare organisations and professionals to support ill or disabled parents. The implications of this for understanding caring within families, and for the role of the state, are explored in Chapters 3 and 5.

How we define young carers and view their relationships with their parents and extended family will influence how policies and services are formulated and implemented to meet the needs of children *and* ill or disabled adults. The definition also provokes a number of other questions relating to caring by children and within families, and in relation to paid professional carers. For example, at what age is it appropriate for children to take on certain caring tasks and responsibilities? Should service providers focus on delivering services and support to young carers to help them in their caring roles, or should they be attempting to relieve children of some of their caring responsibilities so that they can take the opportunities available to them as children? Should resources be provided as 'family support' to families where young carers are defined as 'children in need', or should resources be targeted at disabled parents in order to prevent some children becoming young carers in the first place?

To answer these and many other questions we engage on a journey which takes us to the heart of the relationships between young carers and their families, and between these families and the state. The journey also requires us to refocus, conceptually and in policy terms, on what is meant by 'childhood', on what is understood by 'children in need', and on the legislation that may be of benefit to young carers and their parents. We also consider the experiences of young carers in other countries, for there are lessons to be learned from looking outwards as well as inwards. Chapter 2 explores the policy and legal context for young carers and their families in Britain, and Chapter 4 provides a cross-national perspective.

Not all children in families where there is illness or disability will become young carers. In many families another adult may provide care from within or outside the family unit. The family may also receive support and services from a 'mixed economy of welfare' – health and social services, and the voluntary and private sectors. These organisations work with families as part of the state's policies and provision for community care, or as part of the welfare infrastructure which exists to protect children and support families. Clearly, the involvement of welfare organisations and paid professionals will be critical in determining the quality of life and autonomy of young carers and their ill or disabled family members. The strategic significance of professional roles and responsibilities, as determined through legislation and policy, is a theme which underpins much of this volume and one which has important implications for the planning and delivery of policies and services to young carers and their ill or disabled parents.

Given the significance of these themes and concerns, because they relate so centrally to the quality of life of some of the most vulnerable people in society, it is perhaps surprising that young carers have only recently been 'discovered'. Why young carers have been 'neglected' – conceptually, academically and in policy and practice terms – is another issue which is examined in this book.

The Young Carers Research Group

The Young Carers Research Group (YCRG) at Loughborough University was founded in 1992 and has been at the forefront of working with the many issues that are highlighted in the above discussion and which are developed in depth in this volume. Since its foundation, the YCRG has conducted much of the research which exists to date on young carers, and the Group has had a powerful influence on the development of services and policy responses in the UK and abroad, particularly on the rapid growth of young carers projects and initiatives.

In this book, we, as members of the YCRG, have refined and developed some of our earlier analyses and arguments, including our thinking and understanding of the relationships between young carers and their ill or disabled parents; the relationships between these families and the state; the types of services which young carers and their families need; and the appropriateness or otherwise of children being involved in certain caring tasks and responsibilities. In talking about meeting the needs of young carers and their families there has also been a shift in emphasis towards a more family-based approach. This requires the development of new ways of thinking about 'caring' within families and ways of working which value all family members. Caring by children, and caring by ill or disabled parents for their children, need to be understood in the context of intergenerational caring, reciprocity and interdependence in families.

This volume draws, therefore, on our earlier research and on the work of many other researchers, policy makers and practitioners. It also takes us in new directions, not just conceptually but also in terms of our prescriptions for policy and practice.

Structure of the book

Chapter 1 examines and reviews critically three sets of literature on young carers and their families: the medical literature concerned with the impact of ill health and disability on family functioning; the young carers literature (including much of the work of the YCRG); and the social model of disability which challenges the previous two sets of literature. This chapter provides the context for the volume as a whole.

Chapter 2 considers the policy and legal context in which family care is given and received in Britain. The interplay between assumptions about family obligations and the legal framework which defines the boundaries between family-based care and state-provided care are also explored. We review the legislation that relates to children, carers and disabled people. In our view, the experiences of young carers and their families need to be understood as reflections of family obligations and the policy and legal context for community and informal care.

Chapter 3 focuses on the implementation of policy and practice – how best to support young carers and their families. In doing this we use and develop the conceptual framework provided in Chapter 1. For example, we discuss the debate over the needs and rights of young carers versus the needs and rights of ill and disabled people. The range of existing services for young carers and their families, including young carers projects, are explored and we discuss how these and other initiatives might be developed to provide a more family-centred approach. We also consider the roles and responsibilities of welfare organisations and professionals in supporting young carers and their families.

Chapter 4 examines some of the implications of cross-national demographic changes and trends for family carers, particularly the young. Data is reviewed from a number of countries, including Britain, Sweden, Germany, Australia and the United States. In particular, the chapter is concerned with assessing the extent to which the balance between state provision and family-based care, and the nature of the 'welfare mix' in a particular country, affects the experiences of, and responses to, young carers and their families.

In the final chapter the main themes of the book are drawn together and a number of conclusions are offered. We consider young caring in the context of 'childhood' and 'caring' and the tensions and contradictions therein. Also considered is how professionals might best provide family support to young carers and their ill or disabled parents, support which values the rights of all family members to achieve autonomy, independence and security.

Language

We are mindful, along with many other researchers, that the use of language with respect to carers and the people for whom they care is delicate, contested and controversial. As with others, we use the term 'carer' or 'care-giver' instead of 'informal carer' because carers and their organisations have stated that this is their preference. We use the phrase 'cared-for person' or 'care receiver' instead of 'dependant', again because people who receive care often do not see themselves as 'dependent' and certainly do not like the title or connotations associated with the label. As we show in Chapter 5, the boundaries between being a carer and care receiver are far from clear, indeed most if not all of us receive and give care at the same time, or certainly at different times in life.

We see this volume as the culmination of five years of our thinking and research on young carers. We acknowledge, with some trepidation but also with excitement, that the academic study of young carers and their families is in its infancy. This volume is offered as a contribution to the growing bodies of work on the 'sociology of childhood' and on young carers and their families. Our hope is that others – academics, policy makers, practitioners, young carers and their families – will engage with the issues and concerns raised here.

Chapter 1
Young Carers Perceived

Introduction

In this chapter three sets of literature are examined and reviewed critically. These are directly relevant to our consideration of young carers and their families. The first is a medical literature which originates from the early 1950s, and is primarily concerned with the impact of ill health and disability on families, including children. The second literature – what we term the young carers literature – originates from the late 1980s and early 1990s and is concerned specifically with children who are care-givers ('young carers') within families where there is ill health, or physical or mental impairment. This research, mostly qualitative in nature, assumes a different paradigm from that of the medical literature. The focus of the young carers literature is on children as competent social agents and how they experience their roles and responsibilities as care-givers within family life. It is rooted in a children's and carers' rights paradigm which views children and carers as fulfilling distinct family and social roles, including being the main providers of care in the community.

The third body of work, which originates from the late 1970s, is what we term the social model of disability literature. This literature has included a direct response to the young carers literature from a disability rights perspective. The paradigm governing this literature is a social model of disability which rejects both the medical model of the early clinical research and the children's/carers' rights paradigm of the young carers research. It is more concerned with the rights and needs of disabled people and their experiences of 'disabling barriers', including discrimination and exclusion.

The three sets of literature offer different and sometimes conflicting – even antagonistic – perspectives on the experiences and concept of 'young carers'. Moreover, the implications for policy and practice for young carers *and* their families differ according to each body of literature. But perhaps most importantly, examining the three sets of literature in the order outlined above shows how 'disability', 'caring' and 'childhood' have been conceptualised over more than three decades, and how perceptions, research and knowledge have changed during this period.

The medical literature

This body of work focuses on the impacts of parental illness or disability in the context of family relations and dynamics. The research, from the late 1950s to about the mid 1980s, tended to highlight the *negative* impacts of parental illness or disability, often viewing physical and mental impairment as a crisis for the family (Arnaud, 1959; Castro de la Mata *et al.*, 1960; Anthony, 1970; Romano, 1976), and especially for children within these families (Orvaschel *et al.*, 1980; Cytryn *et al.*, 1982; Mednick *et al.*, 1982; Schilling *et al.*, 1982; Feldman *et al.*, 1985; O'Neill, 1985).

Apart from studies relating to specific sensory disabilities, such as hearing and visual impairment, which tended to focus on issues of communication and learning acquisition in children (Olgas, 1974; Schiff & Ventry, 1976; Adamson *et al.*, 1977; Frankenburg *et al.*, 1985), the majority of the early clinical research concerned with the impact of parental illness or disability on the *family* tended to highlight issues relating to family breakdown, effects on patterns of family interaction and adjustment, effects on lifestyles, life goals and expectations, and role patterns (Arnaud, 1959; Castro de la Mata *et al.*, 1960; Anthony, 1970; Raymond *et al.*, 1975; Cogswell, 1976; Bleuler, 1978; Hatfield, 1978).

Studies concerned more with the impact of parental illness and disability on *children* focused on the risks to children in terms of maladjustment, behavioural problems, and genetic and psychological risk factors. Researchers also focused on the child rearing practices of disabled parents. Studies implicated parents in the 'maladjustment' of their children's development. Thus, to be sick or disabled meant a dual disadvantage for parents, in that their physical or mental impairment was linked with notions of inadequate or ineffective parenting (Arnaud, 1959; Castro de la Mata *et al.*, 1960; Lidz & Fleck, 1965; Anthony, 1970; Power, 1977).

Where a parent is sick or disabled the clinical literature suggests that children will be more susceptible to increased levels of anxiety, depression or fear and a change in behavioural and social patterns, as well as being more at risk of transmission of the particular parental condition. Essentially, the literature describes four categories of impact – acquisitional, social, emotional and behavioural (Anthony, 1970; Rieder, 1973; Romano, 1976; Sturges, 1978; Seifer *et al.*, 1981; Cytryn *et al.*, 1982; Mednick *et al.*, 1982; Feldman *et al.*, 1985). Each category is reviewed briefly below.

Acquisitional

It is in the area of mental illness and affective disorders where authors concentrate most on the risk of transmission of the parental condition to the child. Anthony describes the increased risk of psychopathology in families, but especially in children, because they 'assimilate abnormal attitudes and behaviour' (1970: p. 144). Other authors simply suggest that the increased risk of disorder or psychopathology among children is an inevitable consequence of a parent's mental impairment. This seems particularly true of the work carried out on parental schizophrenia. In this area many authors report findings that suggest increased frequencies of disorder, symptomatology or psychopathology in children of parents with the condition (Gottesman & Shields, 1972; Bleuler, 1978; Hatfield, 1978; Erlenmeyer-Kimling *et al.*, 1980). Mednick and colleagues (1982) even studied the effects of parental schizophrenia in relation to perinatal conditions and found babies of parents with schizophrenia were more prone to low birth weight.

Social

The clinical literature describes the social impact of parental illness or disability on children mainly in terms of social stigma. Romano, for example, argues that 'Children are often the recipients of thoughtless or pitying remarks from peers, teachers, strangers, or neighbours; these remarks may initially mobilise a great deal of distress in the children of a newly handicapped parent...' (1976: p. 314).

Research suggests that this stigma occurs when a parent has a mental, physical or hearing impairment. Children of parents with mental health problems are often vulnerable, 'partly because they feel stigmatised by their parents' disabilities' (Sargent, 1985: p. 617). Hilbourne (1973) considered the notion of stigma by association and adopts Goffman's (1969: p. 499) idea of 'courtesy stigma', referring to an individual who is 'stigmatised by his very association with a disabled person'. So, for example, when hearing children interpret for their hearing impaired parents this 'can be embarrassing for the child, since it inevitably generates public interest and attention. The child may experience the interpreting as another marker of the "difference" of his or her family from others' (Frankenburg *et al.*, 1985: p. 99).

Emotional

When considering the emotional or psychological impact of parental illness or disability on children, the reactions described in the clinical literature are wide ranging. For example, Sturges relates the stress caused by mental illness in the family to that of divorce and death, rendering children 'vulnerable to emotional disturbance' (1977: p. 89). Sturges is particularly concerned with the impact on children of the three stages of parental illness: pre-hospitalisation, hospitalisation and discharge. According to Sturges, it is during these stages that children experience their most intense anxieties, and the fear that is generated at this time relates to fear of the illness itself (if it is contractible), fear of parental prognosis and general uncertainties about the nature and cause of the illness. Crisis is the result of such fear and anxiety.

> 'Every child needs to grow up in a stable environment characterized by consistent relationships. Many children are instead subjected to unending crises stemming from a parent's illness and repeated hospitalizations which provoke chronic uncertainty and unresolved grief that can be more stressful to a child than the loss of a parent through divorce or death.'

(Sturges, 1977: p. 106)

Romano is also concerned with the stage of hospitalisation but particularly in relation to the sudden onset of parental disability. She argues from a family perspective but goes on to suggest that, while adults may be able to deal with the idea and reality of disability, children often do not have the cognitive skills to do so effectively: 'Pre-latency age thinking is primitive, magical thinking, and even into the latency years cognitive movement from magic to rational conceptualisation is a gradual process' (Romano, 1976: p. 310). Thus, she describes the 'staggering impact' of sudden parental disability on a child. She suggests that the non-disabled parent may be distressed and anxious (especially during hospitalisation of the disabled spouse/partner) and this communicates to the child. Furthermore, parental hospitalisation results in loss of 'emotional anchors' for the child and the anxiety this causes may mean that children – older ones particularly – will experience parental disability as a crisis.

In the case of Huntington's disease, Power (1971) found that children either responded negatively or positively to parental illness, although a common factor was a continued state of anxiety 'and the lingering feeling of mourning of the gradual family loss' (p. 71). Notably, Power describes three types of negative reaction in adolescents – 'resentment', 'increased hypochondriacal symptoms' and 'flight' – and only one positive response – 'an added assumption of family responsibilities' (p. 73).

Behavioural

Over a period of four years Sturges assessed 150 children at the time a parent with psychiatric problems was being hospitalised, outlining the behavioural consequences on children and the adaptive and maladaptive ways in which they react to stress in their lives. Sturges found that children adopt 'idiosyncratic roles', such as caretaker, baby, patient, mourner, recluse, escapee, good child and bad child. It is worth expanding on some of these roles further as they are echoed in the work of other clinical researchers, as well as in some of the more recent writings in the young carers literature.

The *caretaker* role is where the child takes over familial responsibilities, either domestic or nurturing. The child may assume the role of the hospitalised parent, taking on domestic duties and caring for other family members. Many authors describe this role as an infantile consequence of parental illness or disability (see, for example, Arnaud, 1959; Olsen, 1970; Heslinga *et al.*, 1974; Romano, 1976; Frankenburg *et al.*, 1985; O'Neill, 1985). The *recluse* role is simply withdrawal by a child from peers, school and family. A variation of this role is also evident in the literature where parents too can become reclusive, as Kossoris notes: 'Often the parents' first reaction is to "protect" the child; therefore, they tend to gloss over the seriousness of the illness or, even worse, never mention it' (1970: p. 1733). Sturges also recognises parents' inability to communicate with their children as well as the silent role adopted by children:

'Parents must understand that children often hide their feelings from their families because they do not want to upset them further and that their fantasies about someone's illness and hospitalization may be worse than the reality.'

(1977: p. 91)

Children as 'care-givers' in the clinical literature

In their review of the literature, Buck and Hohmann (1983) identify several authors who focus on changing role patterns in families where illness or disability is present, especially modified roles for children where they take on additional responsibilities in the home (Olsen, 1970; Hilbourne, 1973; Heslinga *et al.*, 1974). Other authors refer to this assumption of responsibility among children as 'false maturity' (Arnaud, 1959: p. 18) or 'precocious competence' (O'Neill, 1985: p. 260), and describe children who try to assume the role of parent. Romano (1976) suggests that children, especially older children, are not immune from experiencing sudden onset disability as a crisis, and that they may feel a need to become 'the man of the house', or suppress feelings about parental disability and its implications, 'while at the same time pushing himself to fill parental shoes' (Romano, 1976: p. 311). O'Neill (1985) refers to this role adoption as children becoming their 'parent's right hand' and, unusually in the clinical literature, uses case studies and children's verbal accounts of their caring responsibilities. O'Neill also recognises how early in childhood this caring role can be assumed:

'Ken's mother said he had helped her ever since he was 5, when his father left. His third grade teacher said "he was responsible for all of

them, mother too ... he helped Mama alone and looked after
her ..." '

(1985: p. 259)

and:

'Lyle's mother depended on him ever since his father died when Lyle
was 4. His mother said, "I think I used him more than I would when
he was older". His younger sister said, "He was more like the father.
He ran the house." '

(O'Neill, 1985: p. 259)

This recognition of children taking on care-giving roles following
parental illness or disability (especially when it has a sudden onset, see
Romano, 1976; Sturges, 1977) is not described simply as a precondi-
tion of a specific illness or disability. Nor does young caring seem more
prevalent in cases where parental illness or disability is of a chronic
nature. For example, Frankenburg *et al.* (1985) imply that it is not the
seriousness of the parental condition that influences the extent of a
child's care-giving role, rather the position of the child in the family
hierarchy. Thus, the oldest child takes on added responsibilities (such
as interpreting) and the parents may rely on the child to such an extent
'that he or she loses some normal childhood freedom' (Frankenburg *et
al.*, 1985: p. 99).

Many clinical authors outline some of the long-term effects of children's 'premature' role adoption. For example, O'Neill (1985) suggests
that care-giving can affect school attendance and leaving rates, and that
such 'precocious competence sometimes stands in the way of adult
fulfilment' (p. 260). Arnaud (1959) suggests that caring leads to 'over
compliance' in children and 'loss of emotional spontaneity' (p. 10).
Sturges (1978) asserts that, in the short term, care-giving (in the form of
children undertaking a nurturing role for the parent in hospital and for
other family members at home) could be positive in that it provides
security for the child and relieves potential guilt feelings. However,
Sturges (1978) argues that in the long term 'This role can become
pathological in its crossing of generation boundaries within the family
and its interference with peer relations because of the age inappropri-
ateness of the role played' (p. 532). Romano (1976) also suggests that
'role reversal' with a parent can be detrimental to a child:

'Ordinarily it is not helpful for children to be encouraged to do things
for the disabled parent since this subverts the parental role and
reinforces an inappropriate role reversal in which the child sees
himself as having to parent the parent.'

(Romano, 1976: p. 311)

In contrast, Power (1977) studied adolescents' response to parents with

Huntington's disease and suggested that early role assumption can have a *positive* impact on young people:

> 'In witnessing the change of family roles caused by progressive illness, these young people assumed new tasks within the home. Many acted as an "attendant" to the ill parent; or took over, with the approval of the parents, some of the duties associated with the father's accustomed functions for the care of younger brothers and sisters. Caring for the parent became a source of hope, for they felt that their efforts, if not making the parent better, could at least help to retard the physical deterioration and improve the parent's functioning.'

> (Power, 1977: p. 73)

The growing recognition of 'social' factors in the clinical literature

It is possible to detect some change in emphasis within the clinical literature from about the mid 1980s. There appeared to be a greater acknowledgement of the importance of other variables, not just disability and parenting, in relation to the dynamics affecting family equilibrium. As we have seen from the studies which recognised children's modified roles within families, more attention was given to the impact of parental illness and disability on *all* family members. Increasing recognition was given to the significance of external social and professional support in influencing the outcome for families with parental illness or disability, rather than focusing solely on the effect of the impairment itself (Rosenberg & McTate, 1982; O'Neill, 1985; Seagull & Scheurer, 1986; Feldman *et al.*, 1987; Lynch & Bakley, 1989). For example, Feldman *et al.* comment that 'an extremely large number of families who needed help for a major problem did *not* receive assistance from a relative, friend, neighbour or any other individual' (Feldman *et al.*, 1987: p. 150). The significance of support services for families was especially pertinent for those researchers interested in the effects of parental learning difficulties and mental ill health. Rosenberg and McTate (1982), for example, observed how parents with mental impairment shared many of the child rearing problems facing other parents, including lack of support networks:

> 'Poverty, unemployment, lack of vocational skills, apathy, growing up with poor parenting models, isolation from extended family and social supports, lack of "normal" living experiences, in most cases these are the same reasons and conditions that make it hard for persons who are not mentally retarded to be good parents.'

> (Rosenberg & McTate, 1982: p. 24)

O'Neill (1985) suggests that children of 'mentally retarded' parents, although still at risk from adjustment problems, were vulnerable not because of their parents' conditions but because of the lack of adequate support: 'The most important factor in the differential outcome is the presence, duration and quality of the parents' social support' (p. 255). In 1987, Feldman and colleagues addressed the question of how social support systems could help the family with mental illness and the development and adjustment of children. They asserted that appropriate and effective support for parents *and* children could both reduce the likelihood of familial mental illness and help with coping strategies when mental illness occurred:

'Many at risk families are isolated from social support, sometimes due to the nature of their mental health problems or related difficulties. As a result, those enmeshed within the web of mental illness – *parents and children alike* – are often unable or unwilling to respond to their own dire plight.'

(Feldman *et al.*, 1987: p. 158, our emphasis)

In 1989, Lynch and Bakley were more explicit in their suggestions for improving the conditions for the mentally ill, and stressed that what puts children at risk in families with parental mental illness is precisely the lack of 'extensive family or agency support systems' (1989: p. 35).

A further shift is evident in the clinical literature from the late 1980s onwards when researchers increasingly focused their attention on specific conditions and their implications for family life that had been overlooked in much of the earlier work, for example, breast cancer (Lewis *et al.*, 1985; Pederson & Valanis, 1988) and Alzheimer's disease (Beach, 1994; Alzheimer's Association, 1995). Perhaps more significantly, researchers also became more interested in the care-giving role from a clinical perspective, especially when caring responsibilities were undertaken by children and young adults (West & Keller, 1991; Beach, 1994, 1997; Schumacher, 1995).

Much of the work from this period highlighted the inadequacies of previous clinical research, in relation to its objectives and in terms of its focus on the maladjustment of children rather than intervention strategies that might help them.

'Most studies placed emphasis on the patient's problems rather than on the family's.'

(Pederson & Valanis, 1988: p. 95)

'There is a compelling need for more accurate information about a population which has been labeled "at risk": children of ill parents. Health care professionals need guidance regarding treatment approaches for addressing the needs of these children.'

(Blackford, 1988: p. 33)

There is also a perceptible methodological shift in the later clinical work. Although some authors continued to use attitudinal or behavioural scales and surveys, others recorded the verbal accounts of children who described similar experiential and circumstantial conditions to those children in the young carers literature. For example, Christ *et al.* (1993) comment: 'Ed, aged eight, remarked ... that when his mother became ill his 13 year old sister, Ellen, became "a little mother to me..."' (p. 422). Christ and her colleagues studied the impact of parental terminal cancer on latency-age children. They interviewed 87 children aged from 7 to 11 years and found that they displayed symptomatological fear and guilt, and were also often misinformed (see also Aldridge & Becker, 1993a), which often led to misconception and 'magical' thinking among the children. Also described in Christ *et al.*'s work are the patterns of 'role reversal' between sick or disabled parents and their children, as well as a wide range of consequences in relation to care-giving among children (see also Alzheimer's Association, 1995: p. 7).

Although Beach (1994), like Aldridge and Becker (1994), identified some of the positive effects of caring on children relating to 'positive relationship-building opportunities' (Beach, 1994: p. 14), she also found that children suffered many anxieties relating to friendship difficulties, social stigma and lack of support:

'Data gathered from this study suggested that caregiving adolescents were especially frustrated with the transient nature of their peer relationships ... In terms of school-based support, most respondents reported their teachers and counselors were unaware of their situations at home.'

(Beach, 1994: p. 17)

The Alzheimer's Association concluded that, 'This caring role can impinge on the normal desires for freedom and independence in the children and adolescents leading to feelings of hostility, resentment and guilt' (1995: p. 11).

A significant feature of this later clinical work is also its emphasis on intervention and support for those families where parental ill health or disability is present and where children are fulfilling care-giving roles. Such families, Blackford suggests, experience 'a unique lifestyle' (1988: p. 33) and require interventions in the form of 'Supportive and educational groups with families, with ill parents, and with children of ill parents [which] can contribute toward positive adaptation of children to their parent's illness' (Blackford, 1988: p. 34).

Woods *et al.* (1989) suggest that where a parent has a chronic illness a range of support strategies for such families should take account of the demands of the illness as well as 'the relationships among the nature, source, and timing of support and the type of outcome' (p. 49).

Indeed, much of the later clinical research focuses on support that is strategically family-centred, reinforcing the arguments put forward in some of the more recent work on young carers. Germino and Funk (1993) have suggested that nurses should 'persistently observe' responses to parental cancer and that the family context is paramount in this respect. Furthermore, Lewis *et al.* (1985) have argued that:

'Services to the isolated patient need to shift their emphasis to family-directed services. Although health care providers cannot be expected to be family therapists, neither can they afford to overlook the distinctions between family – and individual – level care.'

(p. 211)

Although it is clear that the later clinically-based research has emphasised, on a theoretical level, the need for a reappraisal of research objectives and, on a practical level, the need for intervention procedures to be more family-based and non-threatening (Beach, 1994), the general trend in much of the medical literature, (certainly from the late 1950s to the mid 1980s) was to report negative outcomes for children that implicated their ill or disabled parent in their children's maladjustment. Several reasons may account for such negativity in the early literature: the relatively small sample groups used in much of the research; the retrospective nature of many of the studies; the fact that outcomes were often based on subjective assumptions made by the researchers involved; that there was persistent use of 'identification theory', which assumes that children will identify with their parents and will show similar psychological profiles; and that many of the early studies failed to address other variables that may contribute to the negative outcomes for children and families where parental illness or disability is present but unsupported.

The medical literature generally gives only secondary consideration to children as care-givers while focusing on the parent's physical or mental impairment. Moreover, and more importantly, much of the early clinical work conceptualised disability (and 'difference') in individualised, pathological terms. Physical 'disability', mental 'illness' or mental 'handicap' were defined in medical terms as a loss of physical or mental functioning, and were seen to lead directly to the 'malfunctioning', breakdown and failure of those concerned, including, by association, other family members. The model viewed the 'solutions' to these medical problems as physical or mental rehabilitation, often in some form of institution or more recently within community-based care.

The young carers literature

While the medical literature may have been helpful in bringing to light some of the clinical consequences of impairment on families and children, its grounding in a medical pathology paradigm of difference has become increasingly problematic to contemporary researchers, particularly social scientists. The intellectual and pressure group challenges to this paradigm, from disabled people and non-medical researchers, have enabled disability and caring to be conceptualised in other social ways. The social model of disability is discussed later in this chapter.

In 1991, Meredith observed that: 'Over the last decade, great steps have been taken in recognising the situation of people who care for relatives at home and in meeting their needs for services and support' (1991a: p. 47). Equally, from the early 1990s, recognition has been increasingly given to the role *children* play in the care and management of parental illness or disability in the home. It is mainly due to the work of the Carers National Association and others – including the Young Carers Research Group at Loughborough University – that a coordinated body of research, development and support work has emerged for children who are care-givers.

The catalyst for the sudden shift in emphasis from *adult* to *child* carers was a 1985 BBC broadcast, 'The Little Goldfish People', which was highly critical of both welfare services and welfare professionals in their responses to disabled mothers and their children. As a result of this programme and a subsequent publicity campaign spearheaded by the Association of Carers, a 'young carers' project worker was appointed at what is now known as the Carers National Association (CNA). Since that time, aside from the development of the young carers literature, campaigning work has focused on raising professional and public awareness to the issue, which has itself led to the growth of nationwide support services aimed specifically at young carers and, less frequently, their families. Furthermore, as the issue became increasingly politicised in the early 1990s, an early day motion in 1994 culminated a year later in young carers being included in the Carers (Recognition and Services) Act 1995.

But who exactly are 'young carers' and how many are there? What are their caring responsibilities? What sets them apart from adult carers? Why should young carers be considered to be in need of independent consideration and support? It is to these questions that we now turn our attention.

Defining 'young carers'

From the growing literature on young carers a picture has emerged which identifies several significant factors which appear collectively to set young carers apart, both from their adult counterparts and from other children within families (with or without illness or disability) who do not take on caring roles and tasks. These factors include the following: young carers are (usually) under 18; their parents are (usually) either chronically sick or disabled (or both); young carers' duties are such that they can often seriously undermine other aspects of their lives (for example, their social and educational opportunities, career prospects, health); and because of their condition and status as children young carers have often been neglected and ignored by welfare professionals and thus have not been in receipt of support services. As a consequence many young carers have foregone many of their 'rights' both as carers and as children (Meredith, 1991a; Bilsborrow, 1992; Aldridge & Becker, 1993a, 1994; Dearden & Becker, 1995a; Newton & Becker, 1996).

Although the latter points make reference, in effect, to the *impacts* of caring, it is to the former notions of *definition* that we first turn our attention. How have 'young carers' been defined in relation both to their condition as children and their caring roles within the home? The fledgling nature of the issue of 'young caring' was typified in the early 1990s by some irresolution over definitions. When Meredith began his work at the Carers National Association, children who provided care were defined somewhat tentatively in relation to their duties, and it was these that set them apart from other children who had no such responsibilities. Thus, in 1990 Meredith referred to young carers as 'those children who by force of circumstances find themselves looking after a dependent adult' (Lunn, 1990: p. viii).

Within a year this definition became a little more refined and focused on the parental *condition* as well as the caring task. Thus, young carers were: 'Children and young people who have responsibilities for the care at home of a relative with a disability or mental illness' (Meredith, 1991b: p. 14); followed shortly afterwards with the following amendment: 'Commonly they are from single-parent families in which the parent develops a disabling illness' (Meredith, 1992: p. 15).

The swings and shifts in emphasis of the definitions of young carers that were apparent in the development of the young carers literature (O'Neill, 1988; Page, 1988; Meredith, 1991b, 1992; Bilsborrow, 1992) reflected both a development in understanding and insight about what it was to be a young carer, as well as the different perspectives and interests of particular authors. The focus of the young carers literature is diverse. Some researchers have been concerned with the greater picture of the impact of parental illness or disability on the whole family. Grimshaw (1991), for example, was interested in the impact on children of parents with Parkinson's disease, Tyler (1990) focused on Huntington's disease, and Elliott (1992) and Landells & Pritlove (1994) were concerned with families where there are mental health problems. Segal & Simkins (1993, 1996) have highlighted the effects of parental multiple sclerosis on family dynamics and psychology, while others have looked at children affected by HIV/AIDS in the family (Imrie & Coombes, 1995). Some have concerned themselves with a particular impact of caring on children, for example the effects on children's education (Fox, 1995; Marsden, 1995). This difference continued over time and has also been reflected in practice. Thus, some of the young carers projects have used their own definitions of young caring and expanded them to include, for example, children over the age of 18 (see Dearden & Becker, 1995b) although much of the literature focuses on children under this age.

A definitive feature of some of the earlier work on young carers was the analytical distinction between 'primary' and 'secondary' caring responsibilities (O'Neill, 1988; Meredith, 1991a, b; Aldridge & Becker, 1993a). This was meant to indicate the extent or degree of caring among children. Thus, caring responsibilities became divisible by their intensity, frequency and occupancy. Primary caring was concentrated, regular and undertaken by the child alone; secondary caring was typified by its occasional and temporary nature and may have involved two or three different carers. This addendum to the definition of young caring has since atrophied in favour of a more complete one which considers the *impacts* of caring on children, regardless of the extent and frequency of the caring responsibilities involved.

The shift in definitions in the literature to incorporate the impacts of caring on children reflected the growing understanding about the *experience* of young caring as well as its nature. The Young Carers Research Group (YCRG) asserted that any definition of young caring ought to include reference to such *impacts* (see for example Becker, 1995a: p. viii). Consequently, a common working definition of a young carer became a child or young person whose life was restricted by the need to look after an ill or disabled relative in the home.

While the work of the CNA and the YCRG has been instrumental in influencing national policy guidelines and service developments, the 'official' definition of young carers promoted by the Department of Health still defines young carers by reference to the extent and frequency of caring responsibilities. The *Policy Guidance and Practice Guide* for the Carers (Recognition and Services) Act 1995 describes young carers as: 'Children and young people (under 18) who provide or intend to provide a *substantial amount of care on a regular basis*' (Department of Health, 1996a: p. 2, our emphasis). This definition is important, not least because it is the 'official' definition and the one to which local authority social services departments are most likely to adhere in determining their policies, practices and priorities with young carers and their families.

The terms 'substantial' and 'regular' care are ambiguous, and it is the responsibility of local authority social services departments to interpret them in relation to individual circumstances and needs. Significantly, however, the Guidance does signal young carers as children in need because of the nature and *effects* of caring:

'Where the carer is either under 18 or the parent of a disabled child, local authorities should consider whether the Children Act 1989 applies. It provides a framework for all services for children in need, including disabled children, and those young carers, who because of the extent and effect of their caring responsibilities, are children in need.'

(Department of Health, 1996a: p. 4)

Definitions have been revised and refined in the young carers literature. The term 'young carer' appears to be interpreted with some flexibility by researchers in order to accommodate their different and particular interests and perspectives. However, differences in emphasis aside, the young carers literature suggests that 'young carers' are (usually) under the age of 18 (i.e. with the legal status of children); one or both of their parents (or other relative in the home) has some illness, disability or both; young carers are care-givers often in the absence of alternative professional or informal support; and they are performing a range of duties and roles which, in most cases, can restrict their lives. Although children who are not care-givers may also experience restrictions on their childhood for various reasons, for example children living in deprived and poor families, the restrictions on child carers arise from the interplay between parental physical or mental impairment *and* the absence of support for the children and parents in these situations. Where this analysis differs from the medical model is its emphasis on the social construction of young carers as children with distinct roles, and the restrictions on their lives as a consequence of both these roles and the absence – or failure – of external support systems. Where it differs from the social model of disability and a disability rights perspective (which we discuss in more detail later) is its emphasis on physical or mental impairment being a critical 'trigger' in defining children as social actors with care-giving roles.

The numbers of young carers

Although we now have some understanding of what is meant by the term 'young carer', what do we know of the history and extent of this type of informal care-giving? It seems likely that children have taken on care-giving roles within families for centuries. McLaughlin (1974), for example, has suggested that as far back as the beginning of the 11th Century, the early death of one or both parents often meant that young children had to be looked after by older brothers or sisters. Around the 13th Century, McLaughlin notes that life expectancy was around 30 years of age and that those children who survived infancy 'were more likely than not to be orphaned or semi-orphaned at an early age', hence partaking in the care of the family, helping the 'despairing or over-burdened mother' (McLaughlin, 1974: p. 101).

Today, we cannot be sure of the number of young carers, not just because we have no precise definition of what constitutes a young carer, but because the studies so far have largely been unable to provide reliable estimates. In addition, considering the elusive nature of young carers as research subjects, drawing any firm conclusions about the *extent* of young caring remains highly problematic.

The two key quantitative studies that proved the catalyst for further research and development work with young carers were undertaken in Sandwell (Page, 1988) and Tameside (O'Neill, 1988). However, these studies are both problematic in terms of providing statistical evidence of the extent of care-giving among children. The aim of the Sandwell project was to investigate the numbers of school children involved 'in an informal caring role' (Page, 1988: p. 31) and the effects of this role on their education, as well as some other aspects of their lives. However, these objectives were circumscribed by the methodology employed, as young carers were not approached directly and the data were collected second-hand from school staff. Consequently, as Page admits, 'The survey was only likely to provide evidence of the problem as known to pastoral staff at schools' (1988: p. 32). Of the 16 000 school aged pupils targeted (at 25 secondary schools in Sandwell), excluding fifth year pupils, 95 young carers were identified and a further 74 were 'suspected' of caring. Young carers who only experienced problems from time to time were not included. As the 95 young carers identified were cases already known to pastoral staff there was no way of knowing about the 'unknowns'.

In terms of identifying the *extent* of young caring, Page's study was neither particularly useful nor necessarily accurate. The data was also of limited use to study the impact of caring as it relied on indirect anecdotal accounts. Furthermore, such accounts were also called into question by those providing the information, as one teacher pointed out: 'With students in this age range, one is very much at the mercy of what they are prepared to tell of the situation' (Page, 1988: p. 35). Ultimately, the study failed to fulfil its stated aims of gaining statistical information on the extent of young caring or providing insights into the experiences of young carers (except indirectly). However, it was successful in providing 'information to guide future developments' (Page, 1988: p. 32), which encouraged a greater interest in the subject.

The Tameside survey (O'Neill, 1988) was also similarly confined in its objective to provide statistical evidence on the extent of young caring. This study formed part of a Carers Survey in which a postal questionnaire was distributed to 17 200 randomly selected homes in the Tameside area. In order to identify carers, the questionnaire's 'basic thrust' was to ask the question 'Are you a carer?' This was perhaps not the most effective way of locating young carers as evidence suggests that many children and their parents, neither recognise the child's role as a caring one, nor necessarily admit to outsiders the presence of child carers in their families (see Meredith, 1991b; Aldridge & Becker, 1993a). However, O'Neill concluded that 'prime' caring among children was rare, suggesting 50 or 60 cases in a borough with a population of 216 000. Indeed, O'Neill compared the incidence of young caring to that of road accidents: 'If adult caring is on a comparable scale with unemployment, young caring is probably on a similar scale to severe road accidents' (p. 2).

O'Neill did recognise the survey's shortcomings and concluded that the survey only gave 'ball park figures', identifying about 10% of all young carers. Despite the problematic nature of these two early studies in terms of providing statistical information, both surveys were instrumental in highlighting the urgent need for future work on young carers, the thrust of which, it was suggested, should be more qualitative in nature.

'One can get caught up in the numbers game. One has to look at the size of the problem in the context of the severity of impacts on individuals... It is arguably more important to identify each individual case than might be true for the Carers Survey as a whole.'

(O'Neill, 1988: p. 3)

A small number of later surveys tried to calculate more accurately the number of children involved in caring nationwide. In 1995, Mahon and Higgins suggested that the earlier estimate of 10 000 young carers nationwide may have been an underestimate and that a more accurate figure might be between 15 000 and 40 000. Additionally, through secondary analysis of 1985 General Household Survey data, Parker (1992, 1994) was able to determine that 17% of carers aged 16–35 had caring responsibilities before their 16th birthday, and that one third of these had been assisting their parents. Parker calculated that:

'This means that of the 1.2 million carers aged 35 and under in 1985, some 212 000 had been providing care since before the age of 16 and, of those, around 68 000 for a parent.'

(Parker, 1994: p. 9)

Few researchers have since concerned themselves with generating statistical data on young carers, due, no doubt, to the inherent problems of locating them – the often hidden nature of young caring does not lend itself easily to quantitative study (see Meredith, 1991a; Aldridge & Becker, 1993a). However, a considerable number of studies have employed qualitative research methods in order to generate information on the *experiences* and *circumstances* of children who care (Bilsborrow, 1992; Aldridge & Becker, 1993a; Dearden & Becker, 1995a; Frank, 1995; Newton & Becker, 1996). This empirical shift has resulted in a much more detailed representation of young carers' experiences and needs, very often from their own perspective and using their own words. This would be expected from a qualitative approach to data collection and analysis. The practical consequences have been that young carers now have access to a wide range of support services across Britain specifically intended to meet their needs and, in some cases, the needs of their families as well (see Aldridge & Becker, 1998). This, in turn, has opened up new avenues for empirical investigation, the most significant being the ready access to young carers themselves.

Thus, while the 'numbers game' gave way to the qualitative study of young carers' lives and experiences, and as the number of identified young carers has grown (because of the new policy initiatives and services), the opportunities to conduct quantitative and qualitative research have also increased. For example, Frank's (1995) study in Hampshire provided data on 91 young carers, while Mahon and Higgins (1995) were able to collect and analyse data on 281 young carers in contact with three projects. Dearden and Becker (1995) collated data on approximately 650 young carers who were supported by young carers projects, combining quantitative and qualitative methodologies, while in 1997 they repeated the exercise, collecting data on more than 2300 young carers in contact with projects across Britain (Dearden & Becker, 1995a, 1998). However, where these studies differed from the earlier quantitative ones was that they did not attempt to estimate the number of young carers nationally. Rather, the data were collected and used to examine the characteristics and experiences of a larger group of young carers than had hitherto been possible.

However, in 1995, the Office for National Statistics (ONS), on behalf of the Department of Health (DoH), conducted a large scale quantitative study of young carers which only served to reproduce the empirical problems experienced by earlier quantitative studies. The ONS study found that, from a sample of 12 000 households, only 29 contained one or more young carers. The term 'young carer' was based on criteria adapted from a working definition in an earlier Chief Inspector of Social Services' letter to local authorities:

'At this stage of development, we are using the following working definition – young carer means a child or young person who is carrying out significant caring tasks and assuming a level of responsibility for another person which would usually be taken by an adult. The term refers to children or young people under 18 years caring for adults (usually their parents) or occasionally siblings. It does not refer to young people under 18 years caring for their own children. Nor does the term refer to those children who accept an age appropriate role in taking increasing responsibility for household tasks in homes with a disabled, sick or mentally ill parent.'

(ONS, 1996: p. 3)

The ambiguities of the terms 'significant caring tasks' and 'age appropriate role' become more problematic when placed in the context of a general questionnaire survey on caring. Difficulties will inevitably arise when trying to elicit very personal and sensitive information using the impersonal postal questionnaire survey. Although comparative analysis was carried out using the questionnaire data and the results of interviews with families, it is perhaps not surprising that the study uncovered comparatively few young carers, the majority of whom were living in 'households where there was an adult carer'. The work of young carers in these households was described simply as 'bridging the gaps' (ONS, 1996: p. 1). Furthermore, there were certain inconsistencies in the research findings relating to the extent of young caring and the impact of caring on children.

While the ONS report suggests that the majority of young carers were not caring alone and were simply filling caring gaps, half the young carers were nonetheless spending more than 20 hours a week caring (3 hours per day on average), and 'none of the families indicated that the young carer had any days when they were not involved in caring and most had to spend more time at the weekends' (ONS, 1996: p. 1). Furthermore, some of the young carers had said that caring had 'adversely affected their social life, education or restricted their freedom to take part-time jobs' (*ibid*). The report went on to suggest that the number of young carers nationally would be somewhere between 19 000 and 51 000.

Roles and responsibilities

The growing body of young carers literature has shown that those children who take on care-giving roles undertake a variety of tasks in and around the home, including domestic, personal, social and emotional caring responsibilities (see Meredith, 1991a; Bilsborrow, 1992; Aldridge & Becker, 1993a; Dearden & Becker, 1995a; Frank, 1995; Mahon & Higgins, 1995; Newton & Becker, 1996). Earlier quantitative studies provided little insight into the specific nature and impact of children's caring roles because they were more concerned with how many children were involved in caring (see Page, 1988; O'Neill, 1988). It was only when researchers adopted a qualitative approach that a more complete picture was provided of the roles and responsibilities carried by young carers and the effects of these on other aspects of their lives. Working on behalf of the CNA, Meredith was the first to eschew attempts at collecting statistical evidence and focused instead on gaining clearer insight into the experiences of young carers themselves. He argued:

'A survey might identify a teenager as the prime carer in practical terms, but ignore young brothers or sisters on whom the psychological effects may be much greater ... young carers are 'hidden' carers, and survey work by its very nature is unable to identify families who are not known to the system, or who cannot identify themselves.'

(Meredith, 1991a: p. 47)

Increasingly, research revealed a group of children who were not simply 'helping out' or giving up a couple of hours of their time when they felt like it, but children who were making considerable sacrifices in their lives to take on caring roles, very often when no alternative care provision was available. In 1990, Fallon described a day in the life of a child caring for a parent with multiple sclerosis (MS):

'... it is not uncommon for the day to start at 5.30 am with preparation for breakfast and attendance to the personal needs of the parent. The child may call home at midday to toilet the parent and prepare lunch. In the evening shopping, cooking and cleaning may take priority over school homework. Often a child puts the parent to bed and sleeps in the same room in order to turn him or her during the night. The involvement in personal care such as changing of sanitary towels and catheter management has also been reported.'

(Fallon, 1990: p. 13)

In her study of young carers in Merseyside, Bilsborrow recorded the verbal accounts of 11 young carers who were involved in a wide range of duties including domestic and intimate or personal care: ' "(I) get up, get dressed, go to the shop for the milk and the papers. Get [younger sister] up and feed her. See if my mum wanted anything ... I help her on to the toilet and she sometimes needs all these pads and that like." ' (Bilsborrow, 1992: pp. 27–8.)

Indeed, much of the subsequent qualitative work on young carers has classified their 'labours' in terms of domestic, personal (including health and social care), and emotional roles. The Young Carers Research Group has produced a number of reports detailing both the material and experiential conditions of young carers and their families (Aldridge & Becker, 1993a, 1994, 1995; Becker, 1995b; Dearden & Becker, 1995a, 1996; Newton & Becker, 1996), as well as proposing a charter of young carers' rights (Aldridge & Becker, 1993a). Two studies (Aldridge & Becker, 1993a, 1994) played a significant role in encouraging further research developments and were influential in guiding policy decisions on young carers, as Jenny Morris acknowledges: 'Aldridge and Becker, together with other researchers, have had a significant influence on prompting the Department of Health, social services departments and organizations such as Barnardo's to put resources into supporting children and young people as "young carers".' (Morris, 1997: p. 134.)

However, these two studies, while influential, were conducted on a relatively small number of families in comparison with more recent surveys which have been able to access large numbers of young carers through a nationwide network of young carers projects. A number of recent studies, which have successfully combined quantitative and qualitative research methods, have reinforced the general findings and conclusions of earlier quantitative and qualitative work (see Dearden & Becker, 1995a, 1998; Frank, 1995; Mahon & Higgins, 1995). Both the small-scale, in-depth studies and the larger surveys (such as Dearden and Becker's 1995 and 1997 studies) confirm a number of patterns which have emerged more generally in the literature in relation to the caring experience, the nature of caring roles and responsibilities, and the impacts of caring on children and their families.

Four of the most recent large-scale studies mentioned above confirm the findings of earlier work. Frank, for example, found that young carers' tasks were 'the same whether a child lived in a rural area or in the city. They also reflected findings from research projects in other parts of the country and those made in an exploratory cross-national study *Young Carers In Europe*' (Frank, 1995: p. 38). Mahon and Higgins' study of almost 300 young carers found that young carers who were providing personal care 'were more likely to be the main carer and were involved in more caring tasks' (1995: p. 1). These children were also providing 'conventional caring tasks, such as personal and practical care. Many young carers were also responsible for looking after siblings and providing emotional support to dependants and other family members' (ibid). Dearden and Becker's (1995a) study found that the majority of children were involved in 'domestic' (cooking, cleaning, preparing meals and so on) and 'general care' (for example, assisting with mobility, giving medication), but a quarter of young carers were offering 'emotional support' and 23% were providing 'intimate care' (including bathing, showering and toileting).

Dearden and Becker's (1998) survey found once again that the majority of children were involved in domestic chores, over half were performing general caring tasks, one-fifth were providing intimate care and almost half were providing emotional support. At the time this survey was conducted, the needs and experiences of young carers had begun to be recognised in both policy and practice, following the Department of Health research initiative and the implementation of the Carers Act (see Chapter 2). However, although the results of this survey indicate some improvements in the lives of young carers, for example, fewer were identified as experiencing educational difficulties and absence from school, a fifth continue to provide personal, intimate care, the type of caring task which both children and parents find the most unacceptable and distressing.

It is arguably the performance of intimate caring roles which particularly distinguishes young carers from other children who do not take on caring tasks within the family. This is demonstrated in the following pen profiles (see Box 1.1) which are drawn from the young carers literature.

Box 1.1 Pen profiles of two children involved in intimate care-giving

Christine has been caring since the age of nine, when her father had a heart attack and stroke which left him disabled. She is now 20 years old and lives with her mother, father and brother. Christine's mother has a full time job with unsocial hours, so Christine has always spent a lot of time providing sole care for her father. She carries out many domestic tasks as well as providing both general and intimate care for her father. The family dynamics have ensured that Christine, as a girl, is actively involved in all aspects of care and running the home, while her brother participates in neither. Christine has been performing intimate caring tasks for her father since she was nine years old:

'I did stop showering him at about 14 or 15, but recently that's started again. I didn't like showering him any more. You know, I thought "I want my privacy, I'm sure he wants his", and I'm sure he doesn't like me having to shower him and I certainly don't like doing it. I suppose it was embarrassment. You know – it takes up so much time, it takes about an hour from start to finish, you know, get him in the shower and get him out and dressed.'

Liam is 12 years of age and lives with his mother. He has an older brother who doesn't live in the family home. Liam's mother has 'back problems' which restrict her mobility. Liam knows very little about his mother's condition. He is involved in both general and intimate caring tasks, as well as some domestic tasks. He worries about his mother a great deal, in case she falls and cannot get up or needs help during the day when he's not around. Because of this he has missed some school, although his mother is unaware of this.

'I have to wash her, wash her hair ... I don't mind it but I'm a bit young though, but it's something that I have to do for her.'

Source: Dearden and Becker (1995a)

Why do children take on care-giving roles?

From the young carers research it appears that the nature and extent of children's caring roles and responsibilities, and the reasons they care, are inextricably linked. Aldridge and Becker have argued:

'... the causes of child caring are to be found in the complex interplay between medical *and* social determinants, not least the "disabling" barriers engendered in much contemporary social welfare and social services policy, organisation and practice.'

(Aldridge & Becker, 1997: p. 4)

The 'barriers' facing disabled people and their families are manifold (Morris, 1995). These, coupled with other key factors, contribute to the form care-giving takes, as well as its duration and, not least, the very reasons children take on caring roles in the first place. Such factors include the nature of the parental illness or disability; family structure; gender and co-residence; status and power; and the availability and nature of external support available to both the ill/disabled parent and young carers. These factors are discussed in turn.

Parental illness/disability

The onset of parental illness or disability will be the trigger for some children to take on care-giving roles and responsibilities within the family. Depending on the parental condition, caring can be intensive and protracted if a child is caring for a parent who, for example, is seriously ill with cancer, or it can be periodically intensive, for example, in the case of parental epilepsy. Caring may also become more intensive over time as the parental condition worsens (see Aldridge & Becker, 1993a). In other families children's responsibilities may be less intensive, especially where parents are able to maintain their own independence and control, assisted by 'enabling' services and direct payments so that they can purchase and manage their own packages of care and support.

Family structure

One of Meredith's early definitions of young caring incorporated family structure. He said young carers were commonly 'from single-parent families in which the parent develops a disabling illness' (1992: p. 13). The need for children to adopt caring roles in the first instance, and the pressures placed on them when they do, are likely to be more severe when the ill or disabled adult is a lone parent. Family structure is also a significant factor in terms of the nature and extent of the caring responsibilities involved. If there is only one child (of either sex) then that child may be drawn into caring in the absence of anyone else available within the family.

The role of the young carer can have an impact on family structure. It may not simply be the case that family structure and circumstances influence child caring – that a lone parent's illness or disability inevitably 'forces' children into caring roles – but that care-giving by children can affect family status. For example, there is evidence of mothers who, with the onset of disability, were forced to accept their children as the main providers of care, and that these caring responsibilities had increased over time because the father refused, or was reluctant, to engage in caring activity. In some extreme cases the father left the family home altogether, leaving the child to undertake the care-giving role (Blackford, 1988; Aldridge & Becker, 1993a). This in turn can have implications for the employment and economic status of the family.

Gender and co-residence

There has been no research concerned specifically with gender and young caring, but studies which provide any such information tend to identify more girls as young carers, caring more often for women, usually their mothers (see Page, 1988; Aldridge & Becker, 1993a; Beach, 1994; Dearden & Becker, 1995a).

Dearden and Becker (1995a) suggest that gender is an important factor contributing to some children taking on care-giving roles, but it is the co-residence of the child in the family which is the determining factor in most instances. While 34% of adults who are informal carers and who devote twenty or more hours per week to caring do not live with the person for whom they care (OPCS, 1992), child care-givers will almost always be co-resident because of their status as 'dependent' children.

However, this is not to say that gender has no role to play in families where children take on care-giving responsibilities. In two parent families where the person receiving care is the mother, there is evidence that children are more likely to take on caring tasks than where the care recipient is the father. It appears that where the father is the person cared for, mothers are more likely to care alongside their children (Dearden & Becker, 1995a). The gender of the young carer can also play a significant part in some families, especially where there are a number of children of both sexes who are co-resident and 'available' to care. Girls may take on care-giving roles specifically because of gender assumptions (Aldridge & Becker, 1993a; Dearden & Becker, 1995a).

Status and power

It is because of their subordinate status as children that some young people can be 'elected' into a caring role by an adult. Their position as children, combined with their relative lack of power, leaves them with little choice but to accept the role. From an early age some children may be 'socialised' into caring roles by the gradual extension of their caring responsibilities over time. There is evidence that caring can often start at a very early age and both the nature and the duration of the caring role increases gradually so that some children have very little memory of a time entirely free from caring (see Aldridge & Becker, 1993a; Newton & Becker, 1996). Children may also be 'elected' into their caring roles by other family members who are unable or refuse to care (Aldridge & Becker, 1994: p. 2).

Children's lack of power also contributes to young carers remaining hidden and unidentified, and therefore in many cases going unassisted. Many young carers do not have the knowledge or information which could help them to seek support. They fear the very people who could assist them because of the power that such people could potentially exert. Children's legal position and status means that they have little strategic control over their own lives, and the possible consequences of not caring or a breakdown in their caring arrangements are perhaps greater for them than they are for adult carers. For many young carers, their greatest fear is that they will be separated from their families and taken into local authority care (Meredith, 1991b; Bilsborrow, 1992; Aldridge & Becker, 1993a).

The availability and nature of external support

The level of support available to disabled parents and their children will significantly affect whether or not and why children take on caring roles in the home, and the nature and extent of these responsibilities. Parker and Olsen (1995: p. 64) have rightly argued that disabled parents go to great lengths to prevent their children from becoming over involved in caring, but all too often it seems that both disabled parents and children have little choice in whether it occurs. A common strand of the young carers literature is the focus on the 'responsibilities' of welfare professionals (including social workers, GPs, nurses and other health workers) who have, in the past at least, failed to recognise and respond to the needs of children as care-givers (Aldridge & Becker, 1994) and whose intervention and support could benefit both young carers and their families. Indeed, in some instances, the fact that a child is fulfilling a caring role in a family can sometimes result in the *withdrawal*, as opposed to the delivery, of services to the ill or disabled person. For example, there is evidence of individual community care assistants deeming a child 'old enough' to care (yet with no formal determining age criteria) and withdrawing their support completely (see Aldridge & Becker, 1993a: p. 37).

The interplay between illness and disability, family structure, gender, co-residence, status and power, and the availability and nature of external support will be significant in determining why some children become carers while others do not. In some families one factor will be more important than another, but in many families the factors inter-weave to have some influence on who will become a young carer, and why. For example, in lone parent families, co-residence and family structure are key factors, combined with the fact that most care recipients are women. A child (of whatever sex) is more likely to become a care-giver in a lone parent family where there is illness or disability because there is no other co-resident adult, and it is generally the mother who must be cared for.

Furthermore, the impact of parental illness or disability on family life

– especially when it has a sudden onset – can have wide reaching implications for the future status of such families (see Romano, 1976; Sturges, 1977). For example, parental illness or disability may affect a family's opportunities to maintain paid employment, which in turn may severely impair the family's financial status. This, coupled with inadequate social security benefits for disabled people, exacerbates the family's overall circumstances, as Meredith has confirmed: 'Poverty is an additional factor, it is a problem for many single parent families, but especially so when they are dependent on invalidity benefits' (1991a: p. 49).

However, it is the availability and nature of external support (cash benefits and care services) to ill or disabled people and their families, including children as carers, which is likely to be the overriding factor in determining whether or not a child will become, or remain, a young carer. It is on this point that there is most agreement between authors writing from a young carers perspective and those arguing from the perspective of a social model of disability.

Where children are involved in care-giving the notion of a 'typical' case remains elusive and unworkable because of the many factors involved which influence the reasons why children care. The caring biographies of families are rarely straightforward or constant, nor can caring roles be easily compartmentalised. Case studies taken from the young carers literature (Box 1.2) illustrate the complexity of the interplay between various factors, where family structures change, internal pressures and circumstances fluctuate, even caring roles alter, sometimes over short periods of time.

Box 1.2   Brief case studies of two young carers

Valerie is 17 and lives in a small council-owned maisonette with her mother and young autistic brother who is 15. She has the main caring responsibility for her brother although her mother also helps. Valerie has been caring for her brother since she was five. She has to be there for him whenever he has a tantrum to calm him down. He is bigger and stronger than Valerie and needs a great deal of attention. Up until two years ago her brother lived at home full-time, but for the past few years he has gone to residential school five days a week. However, he is at home at the weekends from Friday evening until Monday morning. He is also at home for the holidays during Easter, summer and Christmas, when looking after him becomes a full-time job. These are crisis periods for the family as he is in need of constant supervision. Valerie also has to deal with the necessary paperwork for her mother and her aunt (both of whom have few literacy skills). When she was 13, Valerie cared for her grandmother who had dementia. For approximately two years until her grandmother's death Valerie carried out personal tasks for her grandmother such as washing and toileting her. At present Valerie is

(Contd.)

(Box 1.2 Contd.)

attending a sixth form college where she is studying for two 'A' levels. She has obtained a provisional place at a local university to study for a degree in mental health nursing. The family lives on income support.

Bafikile is 11 and lives with her mother and three brothers in a housing association house. She cares for her three brothers as her mother has AIDS. Bafikile also has an older sister who lives in a children's home. Bafikile and her three brothers spend every second weekend with foster parents. Whenever her mother is unwell Bafikile takes on the parenting role for her twin brothers (aged five) and baby brother (aged one). She also looks after her mother, especially when she is feeling fatigued. Her mother, who has poor eyesight, is quite ill at present. Bafikile's caring role consists of a range of domestic and child care tasks including helping her mother prepare the food, feeding, dressing and bathing her three brothers, getting up during the night when they are disturbed, cleaning and tidying the house. Bafikile is not a willing carer and feels the experience has robbed her of her childhood. She often has to miss days at school because her mother is too ill to look after the boys.

Source: Newton and Becker (1996)

The impacts of care-giving on children

Even in 1992, when the debate on young carers was in its infancy, Meredith was able to assert that at a very basic level where children were caring 'there can be adverse effects on a child's development physically, emotionally, educationally and socially' (1992: p. 15). It is these outcomes for children which have since been investigated by researchers using, in most instances, qualitative research methods.

Although the impacts of caring are, to some extent, influenced by the nature of the parental condition and the level of support provided to families, the issue of the impacts and outcomes of care-giving remain complex. Although there are young carers whose experiences of caring and responding to parental illness, disability and distress will be both extensive and intensive, it does not necessarily follow that it is only these children who will be in greatest need of support, or that the impact on other young carers, whose caring responsibilities are not so heavy, will be any less severe. Meredith recognised this when he suggested: 'there is growing evidence that where involvement in caring – *directly or indirectly* – becomes a responsibility, there can be serious effects on a child's personal and educational development' (1991b: p. 14, our emphasis). The early studies in Tameside and Sandwell also found a wide range of caring outcomes for children (O'Neill, 1988; Page, 1988).

In the Department of Health's study (ONS, 1996), despite the fact that relatively small numbers of young carers were identified – and that those who were located were 'bridging the gaps' of care – the author concluded that 'helping in the care of the disabled person adversely affected [a young carer's] social life, education or restricted their freedom to take part-time jobs' (ONS, 1996: p. 1). This seems to be a common finding in much of the young carers literature. There has been considerable discussion of the restrictive impacts of caring in relation to children's social lives, educational performance and physical and emotional health. The time and energy children dedicate to care-giving can often leave them little time for friendships or to concentrate on school life (see for example, Bilsborrow, 1992; Meredith, 1992; Aldridge & Becker, 1993a; Dearden & Becker, 1995a; Fox, 1995; Marsden, 1995). Furthermore, some children have suffered physical injury when lifting their parents (up stairs, onto the toilet, into the bath). For example, Aldridge and Becker found that the majority of the young carers involved in their original study had lifted their parents at some time and had suffered physical injury as a result. One young carer said: 'I fell with my mum like because I've got a bad knee. I bruised a tendon and had a lot of shit done on my knee and that so I'm not supposed to carry her, but I still do it' (1993a: p. 26).

Poor school attendance and performance has been identified in many reports as one of the most salient outcomes for young carers. Dearden and Becker (1995a) found that one in four young carers of compulsory school age were missing school, while Fox (1995) suggested that 'children with home responsibilities' have been ignored as a group of children who are missing school. This is confirmed by Galloway who found poor attendance in 43% of children who had caring responsibilities for their parents. These children had been consistently neglected by the educational services:

'It seems quite extraordinary that by far the largest group should have received virtually no attention from child psychiatric and educational psychology services. It is almost as if there has been a bland, but unspoken assumption that absentees who are "withheld" (by parents) merit neither help nor investigation.'

(Galloway, 1985 cited in Fox, 1995: p. 222)

Some authors have described the emotional and psychosocial aspects of caring outcomes, as opposed to those simply relating to children's education, health and social lives. For example, some have considered the 'silencing' effects of caring on children (White, 1989; Meredith, 1991b; Aldridge & Becker, 1993a) brought about by the fear of professional intervention in their lives. Others have considered the stigma associated with caring and with illness or disability – the fear among children of being considered 'different' from their friends because of family circumstances (Aldridge & Becker, 1993a; Newton & Becker,

1996). As Hendessi found, there can be other stigma sometimes associated with gender roles and caring: 'It appears that caring is particularly a stigma amongst boys. Many are probably ashamed to be identified as carers, given that caring is stereotypically associated with girls and women' (1996: p. 8). It is difficult to gauge and quantify the extent of the emotional impacts of caring on children as these are often determined by the nature of the parental illness or disability involved and, perhaps more importantly, the responses to the presence of illness or disabilities in families by individuals inside and outside the family.

There are few examples in the young carers literature of 'positive' outcomes for child carers, although Mahon and Higgins found that 'For some young carers, caring was seen as a positive experience' (1995: p. 1), and Aldridge and Becker also emphasised constructive outcomes for children. These included a profound development among children in their approach to commitment and the positive 'bonding' aspects of one-to-one caring between a child and a parent (1993a: p. 52). However, favourable outcomes for young carers have not been a predominant feature of any of the young carers studies.

Although much work has already been conducted into the consequences of caring for children, this represents a huge area for further empirical investigation. In many respects previous work has only skimmed the surface. In order to gain further insight into the impacts of caring on children and their families, large scale, long-term studies are needed as well as some retrospective analysis, although some small scale retrospective work has already been conducted. For example, in the course of her investigation into young carers in Hampshire, Frank encountered 'Adults ranging in age from 22 to mid 50s who had cared for a parent or sibling when they were a child' (1995: p. 53). Frank cited the example of a 30 year old woman who had cared as a child for a parent with physical and mental health problems:

> 'She was aware that these responsibilities had restricted her own social life and education. Even now she finds it difficult to feel affection for her parent and has experienced difficulties making friends and establishing relationships throughout life.'

> (Frank, 1995: p. 53)

However, such work is scarce in the literature on young carers and, in general, very little, if anything, is known about the *long-term* implications of caring. As the Department of Health report observed: 'While some physical effects in later life (e.g. arthritis from lifting) can be recognised, the long-term effects on psychological and psycho-social development are not known' (DoH, 1996c: p. 7).

It is difficult to contemplate the multifarious consequences of caring given the wide range of family circumstances, conditions and individual dispositions that are involved when children take on caring roles. For many of these children there is no gradual extension of duties concomitant with age and maturity. Indeed, the moderate progression of responsibilities among children that might distinguish the household duties of children who do not have to care bears little resemblance to the actual experiences of children who do. The World Health Organisation (1982) has suggested that children's responsibilities in the home should start with very simple personal routines. In contrast, young carers' routines are often of a demanding and intimate nature. A young carer's introduction to caring is often unexpected – at times violent – and imposes a maturity on children for which they are often unprepared. Furthermore, they have few opportunities to increase their autonomy through the *measured* commencement of responsibility.

Rather than being concerned primarily with *adults* with physical or mental impairments and their experiences of discrimination, exclusion, and the denial of civil rights (a social model focus, as we shall see in the next section), the young carers literature is concerned with the experiences and needs of *children* who take on caring roles, and the impact on them *as children*. Many of the authors in this group accept the broad analysis of the social model, particularly that 'disability' is socially constructed, but their research focus is not on this *per se*. Rather it is on children and their role adoption and adaptation within families where there is parental illness or disability.

The social model of disability

The young carers literature is itself grounded in a different set of assumptions from both the medical and social models of disability. While rejecting the 'individual-pathology' assumptions of the medical model it has nonetheless produced findings which, as we have seen, are similar to some of the clinical findings. In particular, this can be seen in the roles that children undertake within families where there is illness or disability, and in the failure of welfare organisations and professionals to meet the needs of family members. However, despite the similarity of some of the findings, the assumptions governing the young carers literature have more in common with the social model of disability, although there are significant differences of emphasis even here. Essentially, the social model of disability, and the anti-psychiatry and normalisation movements, have reconceptualised 'disability' in social terms.

The 'anti-psychiatry debate' of the 1960s and 1970s reconstructed mental 'illness' as a social rather than a medical issue, helping to dislodge some of the dominant thinking and traditional responses to mental health problems (Laing, 1959; Schur, 1971; Bean, 1980). Mental illness, rather than being defined as a pathological, individual problem requiring institutional segregation and containment, was re-defined by some as a rational response to the tension and stress associated with modern day living, including the complex pattern of relationships between patients, their families and the wider community. Some queried the very existence of 'mental illness', arguing that those with mental health problems had been labelled as deviant by so-called experts, which lead to their segregation and exclusion (Szasz, 1972).

If the anti-psychiatry movement was to offer new ways of looking at and understanding mental ill health, the concept of 'normalisation' was to provide new ways of understanding the experiences and position of people with learning difficulties and other 'devalued' groups. The problems of those with learning difficulties, as for those with mental health problems, were increasingly being defined as the consequence of social attitudes which labelled them as different, and which excluded them from full participation in society. Rather than segregation and exclusion within institutions, normalisation promoted integration and citizenship in the community. Policies and organisational structures would enable people to live an 'ordinary life' (Wolfensberger, 1972; Bank-Mikklesen, 1980; O'Brien & Tyne, 1981; Towell, 1988). This model (or ideology, as some have called it – see Brown & Smith, 1992) has had an important influence on the way in which many people with impairments present themselves.

It has been the 'social model of disability', however, which has had the most significant impact on views about disability, independence and exclusion. From the 1970s, a 'new social movement' (Oliver, 1990: p. 118) of disabled people has attempted to reconstruct the concept of 'disability' and provide a new social model (Glendinning, 1991; Schaff, 1993; Swain *et al.*, 1993; Torkelson *et al.*, 1994). This paradigm fundamentally challenges the view that disability is an individual or medical problem requiring physical or mental rehabilitation (Oliver, 1990; Schaff, 1993; Weitz, 1994). Oliver distinguishes between 'impairment' – 'lacking part of or all of a limb, or having a defective limb, organism or mechanism of the body' – and 'disability' – 'the disadvantage or restriction of activity caused by a contemporary social organisation which takes no or little account of people who have physical impairments and thus excludes them from the mainstream of social activities' (Oliver, 1990: p. 11).

The social model casts doubt on the legitimacy and effectiveness of almost every aspect of contemporary policy and practice with disabled people. For example, notions of 'independence' need to be re-evaluated in the light of the social model. Brisdenen (1986) has observed that the term 'independence' does not mean someone who can do everything for themselves, but refers to someone who has taken control of their life and is choosing how that life is led. The most important factor is not the amount of physical tasks a person can perform in their everyday routine. The degree of impairment does not determine the amount of independence achieved. Morris, for example, suggests that 'It's not the inability to walk which disables someone, but the steps into the building' (Morris, 1991: p. 10; see also Morris, 1993). Independence is achieved if disabled people are empowered with choice, responsibility and resources, and when the barriers to disabled people achieving these powers are removed. Many disabled people do not have this power or control. They experience discrimination, poverty and exclusion (Martin & White, 1988; Thompson *et al.*, 1990). Barnes suggests that there are two explanations for the disproportionate economic and social disadvantages of disabled people:

> 'One is the traditional individual approach which suggests that impairment has such a traumatic physical and psychological effect on individuals that they cannot achieve a reasonable standard of living by themselves... The other, developed by disabled people and their organisations and fast becoming the new orthodoxy, argues that a wide range of discriminatory economic and social barriers prevent disabled people from securing an acceptable quality of life by their own efforts. Therefore, the deprivations which accompany impairment are the result of discrimination. In this context discrimination is not just a question of individual prejudice, it is institutionalised in the very fabric of our society.'

> (Barnes, 1992: p. 3)

The social model of disability rejects the individualisation, subordination and devaluing of physical difference. It attempts to reconstruct disability as a consequence of social structures and processes which regulate and restrict the life chances, opportunities and civil rights of people with impairments. The model also rejects the idea that disabled people are 'victims'. We examine the implications of the social model for young carers and their families in Chapter 3.

The conclusion that care-giving has a largely negative impact on children has generated considerable controversy and, to some extent, a backlash against the young carers literature, policy and practice intended to meet young carers' specific needs. It has to a large extent led some authors associated with the social model of disability to develop a sub-literature, what we term here as a *disability rights perspective on young carers*. Some authors writing from this perspective have strongly attacked any implication that disabled parents are in some way 'ineffective' in their parenting roles, and that their impairment 'forces' children into caring roles or has negative consequences on their lifestyles. Olsen, for example, has refuted the conclusion that caring impinges on children's life at school and restricts their educational opportunities: 'What sketchy evidence there is suggests that the impact of caring, for example with respect to educational performance, is nonexistent' (1996: p. 45), and others have also been critical of the general negativity of reported outcomes of caring among children (see, for example, Parker & Olsen, 1995; Keith & Morris, 1995). We return to the disability rights perspective on young carers in more detail in Chapter 3.

The importance of the paradigms of anti-psychiatry, normalisation, and the social model of disability, is in the extent to which, taken separately and together, they challenge the medical model of disability and the dominant attitudes and social policy approaches to the problems and needs of disabled people. The underlying theme throughout is that the medical-pathology model of difference cannot be sustained in a society which genuinely wants to promote equality of opportunity, civil rights, participation and social citizenship for all. In their attack on the dominant orthodoxy, these critiques have cast doubt on the concept of segregation and control within institutions – the ultimate embodiment of 'social exclusion' – and on the adequacy of benefits and services in the community. The moral and political force of the critique comes not just from the efficacy of the analysis, but from the impetus and contribution that disabled people have made in intellectualising and articulating the effect that disabling attitudes, disabling barriers and discriminatory policies have had, and continue to have, on people with physical or mental impairments.

Conclusion

These three sets of literature raise different implications for how we respond to the needs of young carers and their families. The medical literature is more concerned with focusing on the disability or illness itself – primarily its effect on the patient and secondly on the rest of the family. In the past, however, the focus in terms of intervention has been on the institutional segregation of disabled people, followed more recently by a concern to rehabilitate them into society as part of 'community care'. The young carers literature, embedded in a children's rights and carers' rights perspective, emphasises the need to direct resources and services towards meeting the needs of children as carers. The social model of disability is concerned with empowering disabled people to attain their full civil rights. It requires resources specifically targeted to meet the needs of disabled people as adults with impairments, and to assist them in their parenting roles. These different approaches to meeting the needs of young carers and their families are discussed in Chapter 3. Chapter 2 now considers the policy and legal context for young carers and their families.

Chapter 2

Young Carers and their Families: The Policy and Legal Context in Britain

Introduction

This chapter considers the policy and legislative context in which family care is given and received. It is particularly concerned with the interplay between assumptions about family obligations, and the legal and policy context which defines the boundaries between family-based and state-provided care. Also considered are the implications for young carers. The current legislative framework is discussed which is of importance to young carers and their families, including the law that supports disabled parents and the law which protects carers, children, and children who are care-givers. The experience and issue of young caring needs to be understood as a reflection of both family obligations and the policy and legal context of community and informal care.

The specific laws relating to children construct 'childhood' as a special phase of their development in which they need to be protected and nurtured. Young carers pose fundamental challenges to these laws, to normative assumptions about family-based care, and to existing legislation on community care. This is because, as children, young carers are seen as requiring protection and support, particularly in situations where their security or personal development may be threatened.

Family obligations, law and policy

Cultural beliefs and assumptions about family obligations have a strong influence on the boundary between direct state provision to ill, disabled or vulnerable people requiring support or protection, and between family-based care. The boundary between public (state) support and private (family) care is defined through law, policy and custom (Millar & Warman, 1996).

In some countries – particularly southern European countries such as Italy, Greece, Spain and Portugal – there are strong assumptions and beliefs that family members *should* care for each other. In these countries the law requires people to provide support to their family members, and state provision is thus low (Millar & Warman, 1996). Assumptions about family obligations, and gender roles, reinforced and defined through law and policy, lead to family members, especially women, being 'forced' to take on care-giving roles (Land, 1987; Baldwin & Twigg, 1991). To reject or opt out of this role can lead to being labelled a 'bad' son, daughter, wife or mother, or being considered 'unnatural', 'unfeminine' or 'uncaring' (Dalley, 1988). Because there is little state support available, and in cases where there are no family members available or willing to provide care, a person requiring care can become 'abandoned' in the community or institutionalised.

In other countries, such as Sweden and Norway, where there are different assumptions about family obligations, and where autonomy and independence for all citizens are goals of social policy, family members, including women, have a far greater choice as to whether or not to take on caring roles and the state has clearer responsibilities for providing support (Millar & Warman, 1996). However, even in those countries with more explicit state responsibilities to provide care, opting out of family-based caring roles can be difficult. The reasons why many family members make a commitment to care are due in part to feelings of duty and love, but are also fuelled by guilt about 'leaving' loved ones to institutional or non-family based care. Community care which relies on informal, unpaid family care (care *by* the community as opposed to care *in* the community), by emphasising the positive benefits associated with remaining in the home rather than in an institution, adds to the pressures on people to care for their relatives.

In practice, community care often equals care by women for other women (Finch & Groves, 1980; Dalley, 1988). Most carers in Britain and elsewhere are women – wives, daughters and daughters-in-law, in that hierarchy (Jani-Le Bris, 1993). In these situations the family 'is an important mechanism for the transmission of existing inequalities' due to the division of unpaid labour within the home which assigns to women the care-giving role (Land, 1987: p. 258).

While family members in Britain have no legal requirement at the moment to provide or pay for the long term care of family members (Millar & Warman, 1996), there is nonetheless a strong assumption that family-based care is 'best'. Throughout history, family members and relatives, and close friends or neighbours, have been perceived to be and have acted as the main providers of care and support – including financial support – to those who are sick, disabled, elderly, young, frail or who have other special needs (Kamerman & Kahn, 1978; Ungerson, 1990; Jani-Le Bris, 1993; Becker, 1997). This support has almost always been provided free of charge, as part of a sense of family duty and social obligation (Twigg *et al.*, 1990). Today, there are about 6.8 million people in Britain who are considered to be 'informal' family carers, equivalent to 15% of people aged 16 and over (OPCS, 1992). However, while just under three million men provide care (OPCS,

1992), it is women who are still far more likely to be providing extensive and intimate care (Nissel & Bonnerjea, 1982; Ungerson, 1987; Lewis & Meredith, 1988). Many women carers, like children who are care-givers, experience a range of social and health costs because of their caring roles and responsibilities (see Chapter 1; also Glendinning, 1992; Joshi, 1992).

The central role of the family in providing community care in Britain has been reinforced through law and social policy. The implementation in 1993 of the new community care reforms, which placed family carers at the centre of 'care in the community', was the outcome of more than four decades of politics, debate and re-formulation of policy in response to the health and social care needs of vulnerable people. It represents the latest balance between the state, the markets and informal care within a mixed economy of welfare.

The belief in the humanitarian value of community living has been coupled with a persuasive critique of the failings of institutions for people with physical impairments, mental health problems or learning difficulties, elderly people, children and the poor in general (Goffman, 1961; Townsend, 1962; Morris, 1969; HMSO, 1969; Martin, 1984; Becker, 1997). The anti-institution critique manifested itself in a number of other forms, not least the emerging paradigms and pressure group movements calling for 'normalisation' and a social model of disability, both of which rejected the institutional segregation, isolation and exclusion that had characterised policy responses to the disabled and mentally impaired for more than a century. The social model of disability, as we have seen in Chapter 1, has attempted to shift understanding of the nature of 'disability' away from an individualised medical-pathology model of physical impairment towards one concerned with the negative consequences of social reactions, labels and environments, which effectively 'disable' people with impairments and exclude them from enjoying full civil rights. This critique has also challenged the language and ideology of 'care' itself, arguing that notions of 'dependency' and 'care-giving' misrepresent and misunderstand both the needs of disabled people and their relationship with family carers and service providers (Morris, 1991, 1993; see also Chapter 5).

The Thatcher and Major governments of the 1980s and 1990s became supporters of the process of de-institutionalisation and change. To the anti-institution critique being promoted by many – especially disabled people themselves – was added some of the essential ingredients of New Right thinking, namely that the direct involvement of the state in welfare matters should be limited to support a vibrant mixed economy of care. This would combine the best of private enterprise with voluntary and charitable giving, with family members taking the lead role for providing care in the community. These social objectives complemented the policy imperative to reduce public expenditure on social programmes, particularly cash (social security) and care (Becker, 1997).

Griffiths and beyond

The 1988 Griffiths Report set the foundation for the major changes that were phased in between 1991 and 1993, and which added community care to the growing list of social services' statutory responsibilities (Griffiths, 1988; Lister & Becker, 1994). Having established where the prime responsibility for community care should rest and the role to be played by SSDs, Griffiths went on to highlight the centrality of family carers and the critical contribution they make to the overall provision and structure of community care:

'Publicly provided services constitute only a small part of the total care provided to people in need. Families, friends, neighbours and other local people provide the majority of care in response to needs which they are uniquely well placed to identify and respond to. This will be the primary means by which people are enabled to live normal lives in community settings.'

(Griffiths, 1988: p. 5)

Griffiths proposed that publicly funded services should operate in new ways, and that their first task should be to support and, where possible, to strengthen these networks of carers (1988: p. 5). However, the Griffiths report had nothing at all to say about young carers. At that time they had not yet been identified as a 'welfare category' or as an issue for social policy.

The government's response to Griffiths' recommendations was to accept that informal care should be the cornerstone of any future policy because the family was the right and proper focus for care in the community. The government paid tribute to the majority of carers who were 'dedicated and self sacrificing' and who took on 'serious obligations to help care for disabled relatives and friends'. Kenneth Clarke, the then Health Secretary, went on to confirm that 'the great bulk of community care will continue to be provided by family, friends and neighbours', and that 'our proposals are aimed at strengthening support for those many unselfish people who care for people in need' (Clarke, 1988). The government's community care White Paper, *Caring for People* (DoH, 1989a), maintained this approach:

... most care is provided by family, friends and neighbours. The majority of carers take on these responsibilities willingly, but the government recognises that many need help to be able to manage what can become a heavy burden. Their lives could be made much easier if the right support is there at the right time, and a key responsibility of the statutory service providers should be to do all they can to assist and support carers. Helping carers to maintain their valuable contribution to the spectrum of care is both right and a sound investment. Help may take the form of providing advice and support as well as practical services such as day, domiciliary and respite care.'

(DoH, 1989a: p. 9)

The NHS and Community Care Act 1990 was the consequence of the Griffiths review of community care and established the legislative framework for supporting disabled, elderly and other vulnerable people requiring residential, nursing home or home-based care in the community. The impact of the Act on the organisation and delivery of social welfare and social care services to these groups is immense. The Act provided the legislative context for the introduction of the purchaser–provider split in health and social care and for fundamental changes to the role of social services. These departments were to move away from the role of service *provider* to the role of *enabler*. Authorities were instructed to contract and make use of services from the independent sector (private, voluntary, charities and trusts) where these were cost efficient and of high quality. This partnership with different sectors, the mixed economy of care, was promoted as a move away from the traditional position of social services as monolithic provider, a position viewed by government as denying any real choice to service users and their carers. Social services would take responsibility for assessing population and individual need, designing care arrangements, purchasing and ensuring that services were delivered to a specified quality. The traditional roles of 'financing' and 'regulation' were to be maintained by SSDs; the main change was that they would not necessarily deliver services themselves.

Before services are provided to a person requiring community care (including residential or nursing home care paid for by public funds), there must be an assessment of need. Anyone who feels they might benefit from community care services and who meets local authority criteria can request such an assessment, which determines what care and support may be needed. Within the available budget, appropriate services are then either provided by the local authority or commissioned from elsewhere.

The duty of local authorities to assess disabled and other vulnerable people existed for some years before the introduction of the NHS and Community Care Act. For example, the Chronically Sick and Disabled Persons Act 1970 introduced new statutory duties for local authorities to provide care for disabled people in the community. Local authorities had to collect information on the need for, and existence of, welfare services and to make arrangements for services, such as practical assistance in the home, recreational facilities and education, travel in the pursuit of such services, assistance with adaptations to homes and meal provision. The later Disabled Persons (Services, Consultation and Representation) Act 1986 aimed to improve the effectiveness and co-ordination of resources and services to people with mental or physical handicap and mental illness. Under this piece of legislation, local authorities have a duty to assess for services any disabled person *or carer* who requests an assessment. These two pieces of legislation were the forerunners to the NHS and Community Care Act and they continue to underpin it.

Since community care policies recognise the pivotal role played by carers, the NHS and Community Care Act 1990 and subsequent guidance confirm that carers should be involved fully in the assessment process of their disabled or elderly relatives, and that they too can ask for an assessment of their own needs as carers (assuming they meet local authority criteria). The Act emphasises that *there should be no assumption* that carers will want to continue in this role. It is therefore important that carers are fully included in the assessment procedure, that their wishes regarding continued care are sought, and that potential conflicts of interest are recognised. For example, an ill or disabled person may wish to remain in their own home while their carer no longer wishes to continue in their role, and the provision of services, without their 'informal' element, may be considered inappropriate or too costly. Such conflicts of interest, particularly the cash limits associated with the financing of community care, reinforce the reliance and pressures on family carers.

Following an assessment by social services, individual care plans are drawn up with a variety of possibilities, ranging from support in the home to long-stay hospital care. The most cost effective package of care is devised to meet the needs and preferences of the person concerned within the available resources (HMSO, 1990: p. 27). The major aim is to enable people to continue to live in their own homes within the community. This can be achieved by offering services such as home help, home care (to assist with domestic and personal care), meals on wheels or luncheon clubs, the opportunity to attend a day centre and special equipment or adaptations in the home (DoH, 1993).

In theory at least, the NHS and Community Care Act 1990 established new patterns of mutual dependency among the main players in community care: local authorities became dependent on independent, mainly private sector providers to fulfil their responsibilities; independent providers became more dependent on local authorities for funding; in-house providers of local authority services increasingly had to operate in the same market conditions as the independent sector; health authorities became dependent on local authorities in order to discharge the most disabled patients from acute and long-stay wards; and all sectors became dependent on family carers to continue to provide the main bulk of care, without whose efforts the system would face ultimate collapse (Trenery, 1993: p. 115). In theory, these patterns of mutual dependency were supposed to eradicate the perverse incentives and gridlock that had blighted effective community care for two decades. They would establish the conditions necessary for all the main players and agencies to become interdependent 'stakeholders' in the new arrangements.

Thus, in planning and providing for community care, service users and family carers were to be fully involved and consulted by local authorities: 'All our guidance, and all our work with authorities, has from the beginning emphasised that people receiving care and their carers are entitled to express views about the support they would like, and that those views should be given proper weight' (DoH, 1992). To be effective, the implementation of community care policy required social services to engage in a major culture change, as they moved away from delivering services based upon their own professional interest ('supply-led' services) to a position where provision became based on the expressed needs of users and their carers ('demand-led' or 'needs-led' services). The Audit Commission (1992) expressed concern that valuing the perspectives of users and carers posed challenges to the traditional service-led culture of SSDs, and that many departments seemed to be resisting change.

Research indicated that less than one in twenty authorities had involved disabled people's organisations in formulating their first community care plans (Glendinning, 1991), and people with multiple disabilities were particularly ignored (Challenge, 1992). The Carers National Association (1992) revealed that 69% of carers in its sample had not been consulted at all, and a further 10% were unsure as to whether or not they had been consulted. Warner (1994) suggested that, one year on from the 1993 implementation date, 80% of carers said that the changes had made no difference to them and 8% thought that services had actually got worse. A year later the picture had hardly improved at all: 69% of carers thought community care had made no difference, even though it had been in place for two years (Warner, 1995).

The NHS and Community Care Act 1990, and earlier legislation concerned with the needs of disabled people, represent critical stages in the post-war development of community care policy for disabled, elderly and other vulnerable groups. Other pieces of legislation are also important. The Community Care (Direct Payments) Act 1996, for example, gives to local authorities for the first time the power, but not the duty, to make direct cash payments to certain disabled people to secure provision of their own services. The legislation applies to anyone assessed as needing community care services (although there are some exceptions) who is disabled and is under 65 when the payments start. The term 'disabled' may mean someone with physical or sensory disability, learning difficulties, or who is affected by illness, such as mental health problems, HIV or AIDS (DoH, 1997). The users of direct payments may not purchase services which have not been assessed as necessary and may not make payment to family members. They may directly employ someone – a personal assistant – and buy services from a self-employed person or an agency.

While the NHS and Community Care legislation recognises the importance and role of family carers, the legislation is primarily intended to benefit service *users* rather than carers. Not surprisingly, its relevance to young carers is even more remote. The NHS and Community Care Act 1990 has always been intended and interpreted as adult legislation and young carers have been unable to access it, even while their parents and other ill, disabled or elderly family members may have been able to benefit from its provisions for assessment and service delivery. The same too can be said about the Direct Payments legislation, although here there may be some potential, though indirect, benefits to young carers. Direct payments could be particularly valuable to disabled parents with dependent children if this enables them to buy services which reduce the likelihood that their children will need to take on a caring role. This may involve purchasing services so that help is available at times of day that are appropriate to the whole family, enabling children to get to school on time, to do homework or to join in extra-curricular activities. The legislation does not allow for direct payments to be used to buy services for children. Direct payments are payments to adults to purchase adult services but, nevertheless, they may benefit the whole family if they meet needs usually met by family members. Consequently, direct payments may be a way forward for some disabled parents because they can choose services which meet their needs as disabled people, *and* which facilitate their role as parents. The disadvantage to the scheme is that local authorities do not have a duty to provide these payments and it remains in their power to refuse to pay. Moreover, local inequities will become increasingly apparent over time as some authorities introduce these payments while others do not, and as different local eligibility criteria are used throughout Britain (Becker, 1997).

Many carers have felt that the development of community care legislation, intended to meet the needs of ill, disabled, elderly and other vulnerable groups, has failed to meet adequately the needs of carers. There have been calls, particularly from the Carers National Association, for legislation specifically geared towards identifying and responding to carers' needs. The ensuing legislation, the Carers (Recognition and Services) Act 1995, is of critical importance to carers (including young carers) and is examined later in this chapter.

Young carers, children's 'rights' and family obligations

Policy formulation and implementation in community care emphasises that the family is not only the best provider of care, but is also the most appropriate. Policy and law supports, reinforces and legitimises these family obligations, even though legal requirements for family members to provide or pay for the care of their relatives were never introduced. On the one hand policy reinforces normative assumptions about family obligations, while on the other it accepts that the state has some role to play in supporting family carers, and to involve them fully in discussions about local community care plans and the care packages of their family members. However, until recently, there was little mention of young carers in official publications.

We do know, however, that throughout history children have been involved in care-giving (Aldridge & Becker, 1993a). It is only in the post-Second World War period, and particularly since the late 1980s, that this issue has received some attention in a number of countries (see Chapter 4 for a review of the legal and policy context in other countries). The growing awareness of young carers in Britain has arisen because of a number of complex and interrelated factors, not least the activities of the Carers National Association and other organisations interested in carers' and children's rights, as well as extensive media coverage. Also significant is the developed world's construction of 'childhood' as being of safe and protected status requiring the *gradual* extension of responsibilities. The development of international laws focusing on children shows that this concept of childhood has evolved since the beginning of the twentieth century (Ruxton, 1996: p. 477). The 1924 Geneva Declaration, which focused on children, was the first global charter protecting the rights of a particular section of the community. Since then there have been a number of key developments, the most important being the 1989 UN Convention on the Rights of the Child.

The 1989 UN Convention on the Rights of the Child represents the first international legal structure which recognises that children should have a specific set of identifiable 'rights'. These rights not only refer to those areas relating to prevention, protection and provision, but also to participation. All these, but particularly the latter, are of importance to young carers. By January 1996, 186 countries, including the UK, had ratified the Convention and were thus obliged under international law to implement its principles and standards (Ruxton, 1996: p. 1).

The Convention consists of 54 Articles which relate to children's rights and their implementation. Once ratified, the Convention becomes binding but, unlike the European Convention on Human Rights, there is no judicial means of enforcing it and no individual right of complaint (Newell, 1991). This limits its effectiveness where individual young carers are concerned, but does offer professionals some means of recognising, defining and promoting young carers' rights as children.

The Government is required to produce a report on measures taken to implement the Convention two years after ratification, and then at five-yearly intervals. The UK's first report (HMSO, 1994) frequently referred to progress made under the Children Act but made no reference to young carers, their particular problems, or how their rights could be ensured. It reflected the lack of awareness of the needs of young carers among politicians and policy makers. However, the Children's Rights Development Unit (1994) also carried out an analysis of the UK Government's compliance with the standards and principles of the convention, and they specifically mentioned young carers in two parts of their analysis, relating to the care of children and to play and leisure. They suggested that the needs of young carers were not being realised in relation to Articles 12, 28 and 31: respect for the child's wishes; the right to education; and the right to leisure and recreation. They confirmed that, on the available evidence, young carers should be defined as 'children in need' (an issue discussed later in this chapter).

Young carers pose fundamental challenges to normative assumptions that the family should provide care, and to policy and legal developments which have reinforced informal care (particularly care by women) as the cornerstone of community care in Britain. Unlike adults, particularly women, who act as carers, the notion of 'young carers' does not fit these normative roles: children do not adhere to most current western cultural norms and social expectations when they adopt the role of carer, indeed they largely *transgress* them. Moreover, many of their 'rights' as children, enshrined in the UN Convention, may also be compromised when they undertake long-term care-giving roles. Box 2.1 identifies some of the rights covered by the Convention which young carers may be denied.

Box 2.1 The UN Convention on the Rights of the Child: Articles of direct relevance to young carers

- Under Article 2, young carers have a right to be treated in a non-discriminatory manner. Research shows that young carers do suffer discrimination, in terms of access to information, services and education.

- Article 3 adopts the welfare principle, which determines that the best interests of the child are paramount.

- Article 4 relates to the duties of states to implement children's rights to the maximum extent using the available resources.

- Article 5 relates to parental roles. States must respect the responsibilities, rights and duties of parents.

- Article 9 relates to family life and determines that children should be separated from their families only when it is in the best interests of the child (for example, in cases of abuse or neglect).

(Contd.)

(Box 2.1 Contd.)

- Article 12 allows for the wishes of children to be taken into account, depending on age and maturity, and gives children the opportunity to be heard in any legal proceedings.

- Article 16 respects a child's right to privacy.

- Article 17 requires that a child has access to information, especially information that will promote their well being and physical and mental health. Research shows that young carers often do not have access to information and do not know what help is available. Many are in danger of physical injury, and the long-term implications for their psychosocial development is unknown.

- Article 18 relates to parental support, requiring appropriate assistance for parents and the development of institutions, facilities and services for the care of children and to promote their rights.

- Article 24 is about children's rights to the highest attainable standards of health. Young carers can suffer ill health as a result of their caring role. This may be poor mental health, for example depression, or poor physical health, for example back problems as a result of lifting and carrying.

- Article 27 covers children's rights to an adequate standard of living for their physical, mental, spiritual, moral and social development. Young carers often live in low income households, many in lone parent families where sickness or disability reduces the family income and the standard of living for all family members.

- Article 28 promotes children's rights to education and Article 29 states that one of the aims of education should be for children to develop to their fullest potential. Research indicates that some young carers are unable to make the best use of their educational experiences and opportunities because of their caring responsibilities.

- Article 31 recognises the child's right to rest and leisure to engage in play and recreation. The time constraints and duties involved in caring can make this almost impossible for young carers.

Source: Dearden *et al.* (1994)

The challenge young carers pose to traditional notions of family obligations is further complicated by social attitudes, policy and law, which dictate that parents have a responsibility to care for and protect their children. Should parents fail in this, sanctions may be imposed which may mean that their children are placed on the 'at risk' register, or removed from the family home and 'looked after' by the local authority. In the past such a response has applied equally to young carers and their families. Where parents are ill or have physical or mental impairments, their parenting roles can be made more difficult by the lack of appropriate support from the welfare services and by professional responses that are punitive or judgemental.

For young carers and their families the law is complex and multi-faceted. The position of young carers, as children and as carers, is, in theory, protected through a combination of laws relating to children, carers and disabled adults, rather than by any specific laws relating directly to them. In practice, the legal and policy context governing the support and protection of young carers, because of its non-specificity, is often contradictory. The position of disabled parents is also protected, theoretically, through laws relating to disability and community care. In practice, however, existing policy and legislation have often failed to meet the needs and rights of young carers and their disabled parents, not least because young carers are a recent addition to the policy agenda. Furthermore, as the Department of Health (1996b) has suggested, local authorities are still struggling to support young carers under current legislative procedures, and other more mainstream priorities, coupled with budgetary constraints and the difficulties of locating young carers in the first place, only serve to exacerbate this problem.

There are a number of Acts which are relevant to the status and needs of young carers both as children and as carers. The Children Act 1989 provides a framework for protecting young carers as *children* and for considering whether young carers can be defined as 'children in need' – a label which has substantial implications for young carers, their families and for social services departments. The Carers Act 1995 provides a framework for protecting young carers as *carers* and again has the same major implications. Both these pieces of legislation will be examined in subsequent sections of this chapter. Furthermore, the UN Convention on the Rights of the Child, as already indicated, is also relevant to young carers in that it defines the rights that *all* children have regardless of their status and duties in the family home. An advantage the UN Convention has over the Children Act is that it applies to all children, while the Children Act, although in theory relating to all children, will only ever be applied to that small minority of children who come to the attention of social services departments.

Legislation to support young carers

We have already seen that young carers and their families are fearful that professional intervention will lead to children being 'taken into care' (see for example Elliott, 1992; Aldridge & Becker, 1993a, 1994; Landells & Pritlove, 1994; Dearden & Becker, 1995a; Frank, 1995). Official statistics would indicate that such fears are far from ungrounded as parental illness represents the third most common reason for children being admitted to local authority care. Although 'parents need relief' and 'abuse or neglect' (DoH, 1996d) are more common reasons for admission into care than 'parental illness', it is also likely that these former categories will also include some children for whom parental illness is a *factor* in their admission to the child care system. For example, parents may need relief partly as a result of illness or disability, and abuse or neglect can sometimes be linked to cases where parents suffer severe mental health problems (Dearden & Becker, 1997). There are no research studies which concentrate specifically on this issue, but much of the available literature suggests that parental illness, often in association with other indicators of deprivation such as poverty, poor housing and family breakdown, can be a factor in determining whether children enter the public care system (Becker, 1997; Dearden & Becker, 1997).

The fear of family separation often deters families from seeking the support to which they are entitled under existing legislation. Although parents may seek practical assistance for themselves their children are often overlooked because parents, particularly ill or disabled parents, may resist informing the welfare services about young children, particularly those with a care-giving role. If we are to meet successfully the needs of young carers and their families it is imperative that families are made aware of their rights under legislation and know how to assert them. Since children have been consistently overlooked as carers it is important that families are aware of legislative procedures that relate specifically to their children, both as children and as carers. Such legislation aims to protect children, ensure their rights and, unless it is in conflict with the interests of the child, promote their upbringing within their families. Furthermore, in utilising relevant sections of legislation pertaining to children and carers, in addition to legislation relating to disabled adults, the rights and needs of the whole family will be served. We now examine the legislation that relates specifically to protecting young carers, first as children, and then as carers.

Protecting young carers as children under the Children Act

The Children Act 1989, which was described by the then Lord Chancellor as 'the most comprehensive and far reaching reform of child law which has come before Parliament in living memory' (Children's Legal Centre, undated), proposes that children are best cared for within their own families and that intervention should only occur when necessary to safeguard the child's welfare. The emphasis is on 'parental responsibility' – the combination of rights, powers, duties and responsibilities which parents have, even in the event of care and protection orders being made (although it may then be limited in some way). This is only fully lost on adoption [sections 3 and 33]. The Act also stresses the 'welfare principle' [section 1] which makes the child's welfare paramount. This principle would be applied in any court proceedings which, under the Children Act, are by no means a foregone conclusion. Where they are the preferred course of action, such proceedings should positively benefit the child and acknowledge their wishes, subject to their age and understanding (sections 10 and 41). In the spirit of positive intervention, court orders would only be made if they contribute positively to the child's welfare [section 1]. In these respects, the implementation of legislative procedures should, at face value, not be threatening to families. However, families may still feel that decisions about serving the best interests of the child do not necessarily serve the interests of the family, particularly where parents have to rely to some extent on their children for care and support because there is, or appears to be, no alternative.

Are young carers 'children in need'?

Do young carers have any different or special needs over and above other children? The Association of Metropolitan Authorities has noted that:

> 'It is axiomatic that provision should be adequate to meet children's special needs. It should also be recognised that children of parents or carers who may themselves have disabilities, may have different, and not immediately obvious, needs which should be addressed.'

> (Association of Metropolitan Authorities, 1991: p. 27)

In Chapter 1 it was shown that children who take on care-giving roles are drawn into caring for a number of complex and interrelated reasons, including the onset or progression of their parent's illness or disability, family structure, and the availability (or lack of) appropriate support from welfare and other organisations. Moreover, the impact of caring on some children has been found to restrict their scope to make full use of the educational, social and recreational opportunities that may be available to them. In this context it is therefore important to ask whether young carers should be considered to be 'children in need' under the Children Act. The label, and the status conferred by it, has legal, policy and procedural implications for young carers, their families and for social services departments. When children are defined as children in need, social services have clear responsibilities to intervene in the best interests of the child.

Section 17 of the Children Act states that local authorities have a duty to 'safeguard and promote the welfare of children within their area *who are in need*; and so far as is consistent with that duty, to promote the upbringing of such children by their families' (our emphasis). A child is defined as being in need if:

> '(a) she/he is unlikely to achieve or maintain or to have the opportunity of achieving or maintaining, a reasonable standard of health

or development without the provision for her/him of services by a local authority; (b) her/his health or development is likely to be significantly impaired, or further impaired, without the provision for her/him of such services; or (c) she/he is disabled'

[section 17 (10)]

While the Act does not specify what constitutes a 'reasonable' standard of health or development, there is some debate as to whether young carers should be considered as children in need of services and who may not have an equal opportunity of achieving a reasonable standard of health *vis-à-vis* non-carers. Aldgate *et al.* (1994) suggest that local authorities use pre-determined groups to establish the numbers of children in need in their areas. Such groups include children with disabilities, from homeless families, in low income families, in lone parent families and children of unemployed parents. None of the 60 local authorities monitored in Aldgate *et al.*'s study identified young carers as a pre-determined group of children in need. However, two years later, eleven out of 71 local authorities in a Department of Health survey did define young carers as children in need, following sustained efforts to raise awareness within social services departments (DoH, 1996b). Being defined in this way means that social services are able to provide a range of services and interventions, including advice, guidance and counselling, activities, home help (including laundry services), assistance with travelling to use a service provided under the Act, and assistance to enable the child or her/his family to have a holiday [Schedule 2, Part 1 (8)]. These, and small amounts of cash, can be provided to the *family* of a child in need, rather than specifically to the child, if it will benefit the child. A number of organisations have argued that young carers should be considered as children in need, including the Family Rights Group (1991), Children's Rights Development Unit (1994) and the Social Services Inspectorate (1995).

While many ill or disabled parents may be reluctant to approach local authorities for assistance for themselves or their children, it may ultimately be to their advantage since there is a clear responsibility for social services to provide help, particularly where children are defined as being in need. When assessing the care provided to children by parents, professional judgements are made according to what could be expected of a reasonable parent:

'The fact that particular parents suffer from limitations such as low intelligence or physical disablement is not relevant to whether the care they are providing is reasonable. What is expected is the care which the average or reasonable parent would provide for that child. It follows that if a parent cannot cope with a child because of personal difficulties, he or she will be acting unreasonably if help is not sought, such as local authority services, including accommodation for the child.'

(DoH, 1989b: p. 6)

'If a parent is not able to provide a reasonable standard of care, he is expected to seek the help of others to ensure that such care is provided.'

(DoH, 1989b: p. 26)

In Scotland, the Children (Scotland) Act 1995, in addition to a section on children in need [section 22], has a section on children *affected* by disability [section 23]. This section states that services provided by a local authority to support children in need or affected by disability should minimise any negative effects on these children and give them the opportunity to lead lives which are as normal as possible. Children in Scotland, therefore, have the additional safeguard of legislation which recognises that they may be adversely affected by disability in the family. In this way children of disabled parents, and implicitly young carers, may thus be defined as children in need.

Protecting children as carers under the Carers Act

While young carers may be assessed as children in need under the Children Act if they meet their local authority criteria, their needs as carers may be overlooked. While the NHS and Community Care Act 1990 offers carers the opportunity to request an assessment of their needs, the Act is intended specifically for adults; young carers were not considered when the Act was drawn up. As a consequence, young carers have been unable to access this legislation but have been referred instead to children's services for assessment of their needs under the Children Act. The Carers Act 1995 has closed this loophole, since it applies to all carers, regardless of age. For the first time, the needs of young carers *as carers* can be assessed.

The Carers Act is concerned with carers of any age who are providing, or intend to provide, a substantial amount of care on a regular basis, and entitles them to an assessment of their needs when the person for whom they care is being assessed or re-assessed for community care services. The result of a carer's assessment must be taken into account when decisions about services to the user are made (DoH, 1996a). The *Practice Guide* to the Act recognises that 'denial of proper educational and social opportunities may have harmful consequences on [young carers'] ability to achieve independent adult life' (DoH, 1996a: p. 11). Consequently, 'the provision of community care services should ensure that young carers are not expected to carry inappropriate levels of caring responsibilities' (ibid: p. 10).

However, while the Act imposes a duty on local authorities to recognise and assess young carers' needs it does not oblige departments to provide any services to them. Thus, the needs of young carers may continue to be neglected, even where they are acknowledged, because of an overarching concern with budgets and the management of limited resources.

Another limitation of the Carers Act is that it requires carers to *request* assessment, which necessitates a knowledge of their rights and entitlements. A report on adult carers' experiences of the Act (Carers National Association, 1997) suggests that while the Act is beneficial to carers and, in the majority of cases, assessment leads to positive outcomes, fewer than half of those surveyed had been informed of their rights to assessment. Additionally, of more than 1600 carers surveyed, only 18% had requested an assessment in spite of the fact that the survey was of carers who were heavily involved in caring (Carers National Association, 1997). The impacts of the Act on young carers' lives are not yet known, but it is likely that young carers will, if anything, be less aware than adults of their new rights and, given their reluctance to seek professional social services support, probably also less likely to request assessment.

The major benefits of the Act, as it relates to young carers, are in the way it gives formal recognition to this group of children and provides for an assessment of their needs as carers. Moreover, the Act allows for a wider interpretation of the definition of a 'young carer'. While the Carers Act refers to carers as people who provide a 'substantial amount of care on a regular basis' the term 'substantial' is not defined. The *Practice Guide* clarifies the definition of a young carer and acknowledges for the first time that young carers should not be solely defined by reference to the *amount* of time they spend caring. The guidelines state: 'there may be some young carers who do not provide substantial and regular care but their development is impaired as a result of their caring responsibilities' (DoH, 1996a: p. 11). This important statement recognises the arguments put forward by the Young Carers Research Group, the Carers National Association and others that the definition of a young carer should not be too tightly constrained by reference to the *amount* of time spent in care-giving, but should include reference to the *impact* of caring on children's educational and psychosocial development and how this may affect them in later life (see also Chapter 1).

The needs of young carers identified under this piece of legislation will be met under local authorities' duties under section 17 of the Children Act, i.e. they will be treated as children in need. This will also be the case for those young carers who do not provide a 'substantial' amount of care but who are considered, nevertheless, to be in need of services which will promote their development. Thus, young carers – those who provide a substantial amount of care or those who provide less care but whose development is nonetheless impaired as a result of their caring responsibilities – can be defined as children in need and can expect support and assistance via the Children Act, even in the absence of resources available to deliver services under the Carers Act.

The situation in Scotland is different since the Carers Act there only includes carers aged 16 and over who care for adults. The Children (Scotland) Act 1995 relates to carers of children. Under Scottish legislation, children under the age of 16 are not considered to have the capacity to enter into a transaction having legal effect. The Scottish guidance (The Scottish Office, 1996) suggests that young carers under the age of 16 would have to have a parent or guardian act on their behalf or that they may be assessed under the Social Work (Scotland) Act 1968. For the purposes of Scotland, therefore, reference to young carers relates to young people between the ages of 16 and 18.

Legislative contradictions and tensions

There are inherent contradictions within policy and law concerned with promoting care in the community, supporting disabled people and protecting children. The legislation to support disabled people within the community has been in existence for more than 20 years and some form of community care policy has been evident for even longer. However, in spite of this, disabled people do not have all of the support and services which they require, and policy and law rest on the assumption that family carers will continue in their role, providing additional assistance and support on an unpaid basis. Thus, while writers such as Parker (1994) and Keith and Morris (1995) argue that inadequate services and support for disabled parents result in their children adopting care-giving roles, it is unlikely that, after decades of policy and legislation, this situation is going to alter significantly, even under a New Labour government. The idea of care in the community rests on assumptions regarding the unpaid labour of family members, and this is especially true given cost constraints and the fact that services will be provided to meet needs *within the available resources* (HMSO, 1990). It is this cash limitation on community care which ultimately limits the value of the legislation and policy to both service users and carers (Becker, 1997).

Tensions are also increased because many social services departments have been uncertain whether young carers fall into the domain of children's or (adult) community care services. This situation is exacerbated by the fact that the NHS and Community Care Act 1990 has been interpreted as adult legislation. Such problems can (and have in the past) lead to young carers' needs going largely unidentified in the resource allocation and planning process. It is only recently that young carers have begun to receive official recognition as well as attention in respect of the difficulties they and their families face, especially regarding the receipt of adequate and appropriate services. There is now greater recognition that young carers and their families are sometimes passed from service to service and that staff in discrete children's and adults services do not always work together to meet their corporate responsibilities to families (DoH, 1996b). The Carers Act should go some way to addressing these problems since it recognises children as carers, acknowledges that they may have particular needs as carers, but suggests that the appropriate way to meet these needs is via the Children Act. Thus, young carers will be assessed under legislation aimed at identifying the needs of *carers*, but have their needs met under legislation which identifies them as *children* in need.

A further tension is apparent in relation to the rights of children contained within the UN Convention on the Rights of the Child and the Children Act. Both of these acknowledge the special phase of childhood and the need to promote children's welfare and a family upbringing. However, young caring challenges this view of childhood since young carers are often providing care at the expense of some of their child-hood needs (see Chapter 1). As already stressed, this is not because disabled or ill parents are in any way inadequate or ineffective parents, but that young carers miss out on some aspects of their childhood because of family circumstances and lack of adequate support and service provision. In a study of children of parents with learning diffi-culties, 'good enough' parenting by people with learning difficulties was identified as being directly related to the amount of support available to the parents and children from social and family networks (Booth & Booth, 1997). We have already emphasised in Chapter 1 the importance of external support and how it interacts with other factors to determine whether or not some children become young carers. Social services departments and welfare professionals from health and other agencies have a key role to play in determining 'good enough' parenting and whether or not some children will become young carers in the first place. This is particularly the case where there are no other adult family members available to support ill or disabled parents and their children. The amount and quality of external support provided to the family as a whole will be critical in determining the quality of life of disabled parents and their children, particularly those children who are, or who may become, young carers. The Children Act provides the legislative framework for this support to the family as a whole and the Com-munity Care (Direct Payments) Act 1996 provides an opportunity for some disabled parents to purchase services which will be of value to them and which may also reduce the pressures on their children to provide care.

Summarising, we have one strand of policy and legislation which establishes a framework for community care and the support of carers, and another one which aims to protect children and promote their

rights. Where children are carers it is likely that tensions and contradictions will continue to exist between the two. Adequate provision of
services to ill or disabled parents needs to be accompanied by the
recognition of their children as potential or actual carers and as children with particular needs. This recognition, in both policy and practice, requires not only an assessment of the needs of the whole family,
but also the necessary resources to meet these needs. Such recognition
and provision will enable young carers to remain with their families
and experience their rights as children, as enshrined within British and
international children's legislation. Clearly, within this policy and legal
framework, social services and other welfare professionals have a key
strategic role to play. These issues – how best to meet the needs of
young carers and their families – are discussed in the next chapter.

Chapter 3

Supporting Young Carers and their Families: Services and Practice

Introduction

Strategies for supporting young carers and their families lie, theoretically, in the conclusions and implications of the three perspectives described in Chapter 1 – the medical and young carers models and the social model of disability. A fourth paradigm, *a family perspective*, has emerged as a direct consequence of the debate between the rights of disabled people and the rights of children who care, and is congruent with the principle of the government's refocusing strategy which emphasises prevention in a family context as opposed to protection.

Within this amalgam lies the way forward for the planning and delivery of support services for young carers and their families. Thus, including some aspects of a medical approach, where rehabilitation is the key to supporting adults with impairments, is essential, especially when such rehabilitation practices include children. Some of the later medical literature from the mid 1980s onwards emphasised the need to include children in the reintegration programmes of their disabled parents and this was seen as crucial in the successful 'adjustment' of the whole family to prevent family breakdown or crises. Thus, although the focus of the medical literature was the illness or disability itself and its various clinical ramifications, there was a detectable move in the later literature towards a more family centred approach (see, for example, Seagull & Scheurer, 1986; Feldman *et al.*, 1987).

A social model of disability also focuses on the disabled adult, but on the ways in which disabling barriers endemic in society can be removed to enable disabled people to enjoy full civil rights. It is a strand of this literature – what we have called a sub-literature of the social model of disability – which has challenged the work on young carers and has focused instead on the rights and needs of those who have physical or mental impairments. This 'disability rights perspective' has controverted both the aims and the outcomes of the young carers paradigm. The following section discusses some of the challenges to the young carers literature inherent in the disability rights perspective, before moving on to consider specific services and practices which will be of benefit to young carers and their families.

Disability rights and supporting young carers

The fundamental thrust of the disability rights perspective has been to question the validity of defining young carers as a 'welfare category' and that doing so undermines the rights of disabled people (Keith & Morris, 1995; Morris, 1995; Parker & Olsen, 1995; Olsen, 1996). Furthermore, the response by disability rights authors to the issue of young carers and how to support them has been that, by recognising the rights of disabled parents and fully meeting their needs through comprehensive support services, young caring would not exist.

These authors have further argued that the young carers paradigm has been largely negative in its reported outcomes for children where parental disability is a feature of family life, and that it is fundamentally unacceptable to confer a 'welfare role' on children, especially when such a role inhibits their childhood. For example, Morris has stated that 'it is not acceptable for children of disabled or ill parents to carry out tasks which adversely affect their emotional, social and educational development' (Morris, quoted in DoH, 1996c: p. 5).

The growing body of work on young carers contradicts Olsen's suggestion that research on young carers has provided only limited insight into the nature of child caring, and thus only emphasises negative outcomes for children (1996: pp. 51–2). As argued here, the work that has been conducted on young carers has revealed remarkably similar patterns in terms of the circumstances, experiences and impacts of caring on children. Such patterns in the data on young carers are not only evident in the work of British researchers but also in the findings of research conducted in other parts of the world, for example, Australia and Europe (see Chapter 4). Positive outcomes for young carers are perhaps not a prevailing feature of the work on children who care because the constructive consequences of caring are not a dominant feature of these children's lives or of the lives of their families. This is not least because of the many disadvantages families face in terms of the lack of appropriate support services, information, advocacy and financial support.

The rights and wrongs of whether children should be providing care in the community is part of an ongoing debate within the literature on young carers (see Aldridge & Becker, 1995). Many would argue, like Morris (1995), that children should not have their lives restricted by caring practices. In particular, it is perhaps more commonly accepted that the performance of intimate personal tasks is unacceptable among children (see Aldridge & Becker, 1995). Furthermore, the early maturation that young caring often confers on children opposes many of the freedoms and diversions we commonly associate with childhood and which are inherently children's 'rights' (see Chapter 2).

These arguments aside, the debate about what is admissible in terms of children's labours in the home is, on the one hand, subordinate to the need for formulating and implementing strategies that support young carers and their families and, on the other, ignores several unpalatable realities. First, as we have outlined in Chapter 1, children and families often have little choice in whether young caring occurs. Although the provision of comprehensive support services for disabled parents and their children will prevent some children from undertaking caring tasks at home, there will always be those children who continue to care or who are socialised or elected into caring roles in the first instance. Fundamentally, the fact that we cannot prevent chronic illness or disability among adults suggests that it is unlikely that young caring is ultimately preventable in *all* cases.

Second, children often want to care in some way (Aldridge & Becker, 1993a) so it is important to identify ways of reconciling their wishes with their rights as carers, as well as their rights as children to protection, participation and the promotion of their physical and mental well-being (under the UN Convention and the Children Act). Furthermore, it is equally important to recognise the disabled parents' perspective. Evidence suggests that disabled parents often want their children to care (Aldridge & Becker, 1994), but in the context of security and support and free from fear – recognition without reprisal. These parents want their children's needs to be acknowledged and met without the worry of familial separation (Aldridge & Becker, 1994: p. 21). It is perhaps unhelpful to suggest that if parents are not receiving the assistance they need or have refused professional intervention in favour of support from their children then we should help parents 'see that it is inappropriate to place such tasks and responsibilities on a child' (Morris, 1997: p. 135), when, in some instances, young caring may reflect the wishes of both children and their parents.

Third, the argument that suggests that young caring is inappropriate among children also ignores the huge difficulties facing families trying to access support services, *as well as* the problems welfare agencies encounter in trying to identify and meet the needs of young carers and their families. These problems have been emphasised throughout the literature on young carers, and Department of Health findings suggest that they are ongoing and families continue to experience almost prohibitive difficulties when trying to access support services. The Department of Health cites examples of families who had to 'fight for everything' and one family in particular which was close to breakdown: 'We had to threaten to put Mum in a home and break up the family' (DoH, 1996b: p. 32).

As a consequence of these and other problems young carers have been continually overlooked by the welfare services. The Department of Health findings suggest that such difficulties have been exacerbated by the fact that support agencies are unsure about how best to accommodate young carers under current legislative procedures. For example, although some local authorities were developing policies and projects

relating to young carers, others continued to 'wait' for national guidance
and to see what action other local authorities were taking (DoH, 1996b:
p. 39). Although some local authorities at the time tried to implement
procedures under the Children Act 1989 and the NHS and Community
Care Act 1990 'the conclusions they reached varied greatly' (DoH,
1996b: p. 40). The response of some local authorities in particular was
congruent with the philosophy of the disability rights perspective in
meeting the needs of young carers: 'Two authorities decided that anyone
being cared for by someone under the age of 18 would be considered to
have no carers, and would therefore be eligible to receive the same care as
those who had no informal carers' (DoH, 1996b: p. 40).

Although in theory this response seems to deal effectively with the
'unacceptable face' of young caring, in practice it could be seen to
simply reinforce and maintain the neglect of children by discounting
their contribution to caring and by excluding them from taking part in
discussions and plans about their disabled parents and future family
support services. Arguably, to promote best practice and to serve the
interests and needs of families as a whole, we need to combine the
conclusions and practices of the two approaches to young caring, i.e.
one which tries to accommodate young carers in existing frameworks
and one which focuses on the needs of disabled parents.

Many of the aims of the numerous young carers projects across the
UK, discussed later in this chapter, are circumscribed in the above
philosophy. However, the disability rights perspective has questioned
the validity of these projects. For example, Parker and Olsen have
suggested that:

> 'A more imaginative way of attacking the problem of young carers is
> to see service provision as a response to the disabling and dis-
> criminatory experiences of those with illnesses or impairments.
> Currently the rush is to provide services for children who are seen as
> suffering in some way.'

(Parker & Olsen, 1995: pp. 70–1)

That these projects are fulfilling a need not simply for young carers but
also for their disabled parents is evident in the growing number of, and
demand for, such projects. By mid 1995, there were around 40 young
carers projects in contact with about 650 young carers (Dearden &
Becker, 1995a, b). By 1997, this number had increased to more than
100 schemes in contact with about 2500 young carers (Aldridge &
Becker, 1998; Dearden & Becker, 1998). Furthermore, the Department
of Health has confirmed the value of these projects: 'Specialist young
carer projects were highly valued by young people and their families,
particularly for their focus on the child and for their independent
status...' (1996b: p. 34).

Indeed, it is the *exclusivity* of the disability rights perspective which is most problematic when considering ways of meeting the needs of young carers and their families – the focus is entirely on the rights and needs of disabled adults. However, disability rights authors have argued that appropriate services delivered to disabled parents would mean 'it is much more likely that the child or young adult can get on with the ordinary business of growing up' (Keith & Morris, 1995: p. 43).

Consequently, in terms of supporting families where parental impairment is present, the emphasis of the disability rights perspective is on independent living solutions which allow disabled people to exercise full choice and control in their parenting activities. Many young carers writers would recognise the importance of such a solution. However, it is important to acknowledge the gap between aspirations and the discharge of services. For example, if the assessment needs of disabled adults take priority over children, or replace the need for child assessment procedures in a bid to prevent young caring, what happens when caring is established, when needs assessments on disabled adults have been carried out but the child continues to care in a state of neglect and omission by welfare professionals, whose activities – or non-activity – seem to effectively 'punish' children for caring? (Aldridge & Becker, 1993b).

In this respect it is questionable whether the provision of comprehensive support services for disabled parents will entirely remove the need for child carers when the promise of such blanket support remains unfulfilled. This is due, in part, to the demands placed on an already over-stretched and under-resourced social care system, as well as the failure of some professionals to adopt a family perspective. There are undoubtedly considerable pressures on welfare agencies to provide mainstream services within available resources and it is important to consider the disability rights perspective in light of such pressures. As Sundel and Homan (1979) argued two decades ago, 'Serious attempts to design and implement preventive programs have often been short-lived because of the pressing demand for conventional social services' (p. 510). This is no less the case today.

The Department of Health (1996b) report on young carers signals precisely how much progress has yet to be made in meeting the needs of young carers and their families. More significantly, it identifies how monetary constraints and the need to prioritise cases are affecting local authorities' ability to provide comprehensive services.

'Most of the local authority research findings suggested that the number and needs of young carers were greater than the available resources to meet the needs ... concerns about expectations were widespread and some local research projects found local authority departments with heavy existing case loads unwilling to take on young carers as a policy issue at all.'

(DoH, 1996b: p. 42)

Although the role of young carers would inevitably be reduced by the provision of extensive support services for their disabled parents, it is important to recognise that, in the context of an increasingly pressurised and residual welfare system, characterised by cash-limits, rationing procedures, uncertainty and charges for social care, family carers are going to be expected to continue their support.

The dialogue that has developed between the disability rights and young carers perspectives has had some theoretical impact in that it has served to advance the debate on young carers and how best to serve their needs and those of their families. Indeed some disability rights authors now agree that 'it is valid and important to do research concerning the lives of children whose experiences may be different from those for whom disability does not impinge on family life' (Morris, 1997: p. 134).

The young carers perspective

The debate between disability rights and the young carers paradigm is essentially about a conflict of 'rights', between those of disabled people and children who care. While the disability rights perspective focuses solely on the needs and rights of disabled people (usually parents), the young carers perspective, both at a theoretical and a policy level, has embraced a children's rights philosophy, but not in the context of exclusivity. Indeed, Aldridge and Becker (1996) have argued that the debate between the two philosophies should not be antipathetic. The work of the Young Carers Research Group has emphasised the need for young carers to have full access to their rights both as children and as carers (but not to the exclusion of, or priority over, their disabled parents). This has been a purposive strategy for several reasons: young carers' exclusion from policy and practice; the tradition of omission by researchers looking at the experiences and needs of informal (adult) carers; and the lack of access experienced by young carers to appropriate advocacy and support.

Initially, the focus on the rights of young carers emerged from investigations which highlighted their isolation and neglect by the welfare services (see Chapter 1). Emphasising young carers' rights as children was a positive move towards ensuring their inclusion in service provision and policy. The distinction drawn between children as carers and their disabled parents or other (informal) adult carers signalled a determined move to prevent the further discrimination of young carers through omission. It was clear that, although children had undoubtedly contributed to the provision of family care in the community throughout the ages (see McLaughlin, 1974), until the debate on young carers got underway in the early 1990s, child carers were excluded from both policy on carers and from the research and literature on informal care. Indeed, with reference to the latter, the carers literature has been labelled a 'literature of omission' (see Aldridge & Becker, 1993a) for its lack of reference to age as a determining feature of informal caring. Indeed, Twigg *et al.* (1990) suggest that it is important to perceive carers not as a homogeneous group, but to respect particular distinctions. However, this omission persists as authors continue to neglect the young caring dimension in discussions about family and community care (see for example, Nolan *et al.*, 1996; Powell & Kocher, 1996; Nocon & Qureshi, 1996; Barnes, 1997).

In policy terms young carers' needs have, until recently, been met neither by the Children Act 1989 nor the community care legislation, and they have also consistently fallen through the gap between adult and children's services (see Chapter 2). However, thanks to campaigning strategies and awareness-raising schemes by the Carers National Association, the Young Carers Research Group, Barnardo's and others, young carers are now included in the Carers (Recognition and Services) Act 1995. In spite of this, though, there is evidence to suggest that young carers continue to be overlooked despite the best efforts of the welfare services, and it may be some time before this situation changes. For example, the Department of Health's study, which investigated local authorities' policies on young carers, found that problems still prevailed relating to the accommodation of young carers in current legislation:

> '[local authorities] were concerned whether their existing frameworks could easily accommodate young carers and whether it required more than small changes to existing services.'

> (DoH, 1996b: p. 40)

Moreover, a study of the impact of the Carers Act on young carers (Dearden & Becker, 1998) found that, of 2300 young carers supported by projects, only 12% had received any form of assessment. Of those assessed, some had been assessed under the Children Act (but often these related to child protection issues rather than to children in need), others had received a carer's assessment, and others still had been assessed under both pieces of legislation.

Young carers are at a dual disadvantage in that they are often unaware they have rights as children and as carers, and are often even less knowledgeable about how to demand that their rights are upheld. In addition, if policy and services cannot meet their needs then their plight is exacerbated. Until very recently, young carers had no lobby, no academic or professional bodies interested in their needs, nor did they have any movement of their own from which to air their views and concerns. The young carers literature, both in theory and in its practical recommendations, has tried to ensure young carers' needs are met on the basis of their fundamental rights as children and as carers.

A family perspective

Advances in the debate about young carers and their families and how best to support them have meant that attention has increasingly focused on a *family* perspective. This is congruent with the response from client (or non-client) groups (i.e. young carers and their families, whether in receipt of support services or otherwise). Young caring is not undertaken in isolation from the family. For example, a child's reaction to an external dynamic, such as intervention or potential intervention from the welfare services, may not be simply an individual response (although worthy of individual attention and support) but a family one (see Aldridge & Becker, 1993a, 1994). Although young carers need support for themselves, they also need to be considered in the context of the whole family when interventions are planned and implemented.

This shift of emphasis is echoed by other authors, as well as policy makers, who call for a family approach to welfare provision. For example, the Department of Health has stressed the importance of adopting a family perspective when considering the needs of young carers. They make reference to the Chief Inspector's letter to directors of social services departments (C1(95)12): 'Where the disabled person is a parent, it is essential that the community care assessment focuses on the family and considers how to support the parent and recognise the needs of any young carers (DoH, 1996c: p. 17).

In a follow-up study, the Department of Health emphasised more emphatically the need to 'Listen to what families are saying about the kind of help they want' (1996b: p. 22) as well as to 'Seek to secure, at all levels and across agencies (including chief executives and members), understanding of young caring and the value of a whole family approach' (DoH, 1996b: p. 17). Indeed, the Department of Health has produced a checklist to encourage professionals to adopt a whole family approach (Box 3.1). This emphasis on the needs of the family also finds its parallels in the government's call for a 'refocusing' strategy, from one which prioritises issues of *protection* to one which has a stronger focus on *prevention*. Talking at a conference hosted by the Department of Health (26 September 1996), the then Health Minister, Simon Burns said: 'Research tells us that children are generally well protected when there are serious child abuse concerns. The challenge for us all now is to extend that successful collaboration to wider work in support of children *and their families in need*' (DoH press release, 1996, our emphasis). This is a theme discussed in more detail in Chapter 5.

Box 3.1 Department of Health action checklist: whole family approach

- Start with the needs of the family/disabled or ill parent, and see what needs remain for the child.
- Work with the child as part of the family unit.
- Acknowledge the rights of the child including the right to information, to be listened to and to stop physically caring.
- Recognise that poverty and disabling environments, services and attitudes can limit adults' ability to parent.
- Acknowledge the distinction between *parenting* and *parental activity*.
- Recognise that time spent in counselling, talking and therapeutic work can prevent inappropriate and expensive crisis responses.
- Focus more on support for children in need rather than on protection of children at risk.
- Acknowledge young carers' legitimate concerns about professionals' attitudes and insensitivity and their fear of professional intervention.
- Remember 'families do their best'. Start with the family's solution and work with any dilemmas and contradictions.

Source: Department of Health (1996c: p. 16)

In practice, many young carers projects are also embracing this family philosophy in their approach to meeting the needs of young carers and their families. For example, the St Helen's young carers project echoes the aims and aspirations of many other such projects in its intention to 'acknowledge and value diversity in family life', and in setting up a family support group 'based on the principle of self-help to enable families to enjoy life together or with others with similar interests' (Aldridge & Becker, 1998).

As well as young carers projects, a further solution to meeting the needs of young carers from a family perspective would be family centres and family group conferences. The practical applications of these will be discussed later in this chapter.

Although young caring is an inevitable social reality (as we cannot prevent either chronic parental illness or disability, or ensure that welfare organisations and professionals always operate in a truly empowering and demand-led way), promoting a family approach to serve the best interests of young carers and their families emphasises the importance of family autonomy and family rights. It shifts the focus away from children's and disabled people's rights and towards the *interactive* needs and rights of the whole family. Of course, there will be times when there are conflicts between an individual's rights and their responsibilities towards other family members. How these conflicts can be reconciled or managed, and the ways in which families can be assisted with their decision-making, are discussed later in this chapter.

Meeting the needs of young carers and their families – ways forward

As the needs and experiences of young carers and their families continue to be recorded in research studies, the findings of these studies consistently reflect the patterns in much of the earlier young carers literature (see Chapter 1). One of the most recent studies on young carers and their families is the Department of Health's *Young Carers: Making A Start* publication (1996b). Once again, the data recorded here reaffirm those in much of the young carers literature. The circumstances and experiences of young carers and their families reflected general trends, as did the impacts of caring on children. The emotional concerns of both parents and children were highlighted, as was the stigma associated with caring and disability, the social constraints on young carers and the evidence of school absenteeism due to inadequate professional support. In addition, there were the reported difficulties for families in accessing support services and, conversely, those difficulties experienced by welfare professionals in identifying young carers and thus meeting their needs.

The recommendations for meeting the needs of young carers (see Aldridge & Becker, 1993a, 1994; Dearden & Becker, 1995a) remain in essence both significant and apposite. However, proposals for meeting the needs of young carers *and their families* need to be theoretically readdressed in light of the various influences on the young carers debate, especially since the emergence of the more recent 'family approach'. Although it is still crucial that young carers have access to support for themselves, in the form of practical assistance, personal help, such as counselling or befriending or advocacy, and recognition of their rights both as children and as carers, it is also important that young carers' needs – and the needs of disabled parents – are addressed in the context of the whole family.

With this in mind young carers and their families require recognition of two sets of needs and rights: those of young carers and those of their disabled parent(s); needs assessments for both; intervention to assess needs and to utilise appropriate services that are benign, sensitively managed and based on the principle of listening to the needs of the whole family; and the provision of services which may simply be for the parent alone in order to relieve or prevent child caring, for the young carer, or for both (depending on the family's expressed needs). Young carers projects and family centres will have a key role to play here. The provision of information will also be an essential component of any service delivery to young carers and their families.

Recognition of needs and rights: assessment

Young carers have rights, enshrined in law, both as children and as carers (Chapter 2), and much of the young carers literature has embraced a children's rights philosophy. Aldridge and Becker (1993a) defined a set of rights for young carers which included their rights as children to freedom from harm and to a secure and stable childhood environment in order to best facilitate personal growth and development. It is clear from much of the literature on young carers that caring roles can often serve to compromise these rights, particularly where there is inadequate or inappropriate professional support for parents, children or both. Thus, young carers' rights as carers would include the right to support, advocacy, information, counselling and other services as indicated above. Furthermore, these children should also have the right to continue or stop caring if that is what they and their families want.

While recognising families' rights to sustain young caring, it is important that this is done in the context of genuine choice for children and one which ensures that the impacts of caring on children are not restrictive or damaging. In short, welfare professionals should not intervene aggressively in families' lives to ensure that children return to non-carer status. The welfare services should, as far as possible, aim to remove the *need* for established caring practices among children in families by the provision of appropriate support services for the whole family.

Disabled people also have rights to independence, participation, inclusion, freedom from discrimination and injustice, as well as to alternative professionalised forms of care provision. Their rights can be met in legislation under the NHS and Community Care Act 1990, the Disabled Persons Act 1986 and the Chronically Sick and Disabled Persons Act 1970 (see Chapter 2).

An important right for both young carers and their disabled parents is the right to assessment. Two pieces of legislation are especially pertinent to the needs of young carers – the Children Act 1989 and the Carers (Recognition and Services) Act 1995. The former seeks to protect children's best interests and promote their welfare, while the Carers Act provides young carers with the right to a needs assessment as the carer of someone who is ill or disabled. The Department of Health (1996b) found that some local authorities had also tried to make use of the Disability and Discrimination Act 1995 and the UN Convention on the Rights of the Child in their response to young carers. The Department of Health has provided a checklist to help professionals determine the service needs of young carers and their families (Box 3.2).

Children should also have the right to be included in family discussions about needs, assessments, service provision and the rehabilitation programmes of their disabled parent(s). From a medical perspective, for example, it has been suggested that it helps family cohesion if children are included in discussions and plans about coping with and managing family illness and disability from diagnosis to treatment and rehabilitation (see Sturges, 1978). If children whose

Box 3.2   In determining the service needs of young carers/family with illness or disability, assessors may want to ask:

- Is the illness/disability stable or changing: deteriorating or improving?
- Are the helping tasks of the child acceptable within the family/cultural context, and how do other family members help?
- Are the helping tasks required of a personal or practical nature?
- Is the health or welfare of the child impaired because of the task undertaken?
- Do financial problems affect the family's ability to deal with the situation (is advice on welfare benefits needed)?
- What is the level of wider family support?
- Does poor housing affect the family's ability to deal with the situation?
- Is the parent/child relationship [parenting] good enough?
- Is the young person making a positive decision to be or not to be a carer?
- Does the family have time, individually and collectively, away from the demands of the illness/disability?
- Is the child able to participate in school/social activities?
- Is the child's social, emotional or behavioural development affected?
- Which parenting tasks is the adult restricted in undertaking and which does she/he want to carry out her/himself?

Source: Department of Health (1996b: p. 20)

parents are ill or disabled are included in consultations with welfare professionals then it may be possible that some children are prevented from being drawn unwittingly or otherwise into caring roles, and families may feel more encouraged to seek further help or support if young caring becomes an option in the future.

Intervention at the point of assessment must be positive, non-threatening and sensitively managed. One of the biggest factors in determining whether families approach services has been the fear of what will happen following professional intervention. This has been a consistent finding in much of the young carers literature (see Meredith, 1991a; Aldridge & Becker, 1994). Hardiker *et al.* have rightly pointed out that intervention in families 'is not always benign' (1991: p. 349). Furthermore, evidence from the Department of Health also suggests that the fear of professional mediation is prevalent among families and that it is still the 'biggest factor affecting the identification of young carers' (DoH, 1996b: p. 42). There is also evidence to suggest that this situation not only refers to young carers and their families in Britain, but also much further afield (see Chapter 4 for an international context).

A solution to this problem lies in implementing strategies to improve the image of social work practices and to enhance the profile of professional agencies across the board, from that which is perhaps threatening to family status to one which encourages a positive response to families in need of support. The Department of Health is keen to encourage such a shift in emphasis:

> 'Discussions are underway with the Department of Health to consider how children's services can meet the challenge of the research on child protection, moving from a reactive, crisis-driven service to one that safeguards and promotes the welfare of children in need within their own families.'

> (DoH, 1996b: p. 28)

The provision of services

Support services for young carers and their families may take many forms. They may be child-focused, adult centred, or both and will involve many key agencies within the statutory and voluntary services. Children may need support which relates to their status as children, their roles as carers or both. It could be in the form of group discussion (for example with other young carers), personal counselling or befriending. In any respect children need to be allowed to discuss their fears and anxieties, and require help to develop strategies for coping with their particular circumstances.

Disabled parents may need practical assistance (domestic help, respite care, meals on wheels, equipment and adaptations, etc.) or emotional support, either for themselves or with respect to their children (counselling, parenting support, education services). They may also require services that relate to their children's role as carer (respite care, young carers projects, support services to alleviate young caring). Support may be family orientated (family therapy or counselling, family activities, etc.) and young carers projects and family centres will be important in this respect.

Young carers projects

An important support service which has been designed specifically for young carers and their families is the *young carers project*, of which there are now more than one hundred across the UK. Although disability rights authors have challenged the relevance of such projects, they have been valued highly by young carers and their families alike. Furthermore, such projects have also been 'equally valued by professionals' (DoH, 1996b: p. 34) for their 'specialist' response to the needs of young carers and their families, as a way of locating appropriate access to statutory services and raising the profile of young carers.

Support for young carers has been something of a growth area throughout the 1990s with a remarkable expansion of designated young carers projects, from two in 1992 to 37 in 1995, to more than

100 two years later (Dearden & Becker, 1995b; Aldridge & Becker, 1998). This represents an average of one project developed each month between 1992 and 1995, and the rate of development has increased since then.

The projects all take the support of children as their focus but, by intervening and supporting the child, they are able to make a difference to the life of the whole family. To overcome the fear which many families associate with professional social work intervention (Elliott, 1992; Aldridge & Becker, 1993a, 1994; Landells & Pritlove, 1994; Dearden & Becker, 1995a; Frank, 1995; DoH, 1996b), project workers can act as advocate and service arranger to assist the families so that they can receive the services to which they may be entitled. For those families who continue to refuse or resist social work or other professional support, or for those not entitled to assistance, the support of a project can be invaluable to the child because of the additional functions they serve, such as befriending, counselling and arranging leisure activities. National surveys show that in 1995, one fifth of young carers supported by projects were in receipt of *no other services*, either for themselves or other family members (Dearden & Becker, 1995a). By 1997, this figure had risen to one third (Dearden & Becker, 1998). Department of Health research also confirms the lack of social services support for many families where children act as carers (ONS, 1996; DoH, 1996b). Thus, without the support of designated projects a large number of families would have no outside support at all.

Young carers projects are just one means of supporting young carers and their families. However, they are the *only* type of support provision which recognises the particular experiences and needs of young carers. Services for disabled people tend to focus on providing support for the care recipient and often overlook the needs of children in this context. Young carers do have specific needs associated with their caring roles and the provision of child-centred services can alleviate some of their problems. Furthermore, these projects can also assist ill and disabled parents to access support services for themselves and the wider family, as well as giving parents some 'free time'.

Young carers projects should operate alongside and complement support services for ill and disabled people. The existence of such projects should not encourage statutory organisations away from their duties to provide or arrange services to ill or disabled people and children in need. Furthermore, it is important that young carers projects do not become 'a dumping ground for all young carer/family problems by social workers and others who do not know what else to do' (Department of Health, 1996b: p. 35).

As social workers are the main agents of referral to projects (Dearden & Becker, 1995a, 1998) the assignment of designated workers within social services should ensure that appropriate referrals are made to projects. This is a recent phenomenon in the support of young carers.

Such workers can also assist families by bridging the gap between adult and children's services, ensuring that both care recipients and young carers have their needs assessed. Box 3.3 includes information and data on the UK's young carers projects.

Box 3.3   Young carers projects in the UK

The first two young carers projects were set up in Merseyside in 1992, following research in that area (Bilsborrow, 1992). These projects, funded by statutory sources but located within the voluntary sector, became the forerunners to the many and varied support services which now exist for young carers and their families. They also provided a model for new projects, while establishing themselves as innovative and independent schemes designed to meet local needs.

Most young carers projects today are what we would term generic in that they are available to *all* young carers in a given locality, regardless of the nature of the illness or disability of the person receiving care and the relationships involved. There are, however, one or two projects whose aims are more specific. For example, in Leeds there is a project specifically for children caring for someone with mental health problems. This project has developed as a direct result of local work and interest in relation to children of parents with mental health problems (Elliott, 1992; Landells & Pritlove, 1994). The project is located within the voluntary sector and is funded via the Mental Illness Specific Grant – that part of community care funding set aside for mental health provision.

While all projects support children, regardless of background, there are also two projects specifically for young carers from ethnic minorities, one in Manchester, based within an organisation which provides services to black young people, and another in London, based in an Asian carers' project. National surveys of young carers supported by designated projects have indicated that black young carers are receiving support but that some projects find it difficult to make contact with ethnic minority communities (Dearden & Becker, 1995a, 1998). The Greater Manchester Black Young Carers Working Group suggest that 'Black young carers need specific not special service provision' (1996: p. 6) but also argue that 'All too often providing services for black people is viewed as problematic or responded to in a tokenistic way. This can lead to the assumption that the black community is a homogeneous group' (1996: p. 7). The experiences and advice of projects such as these may assist other projects in supporting black young carers and meeting their needs in a culturally sensitive and appropriate way.

Location of projects
The first ever young carers projects were located within the voluntary sector, and this trend continued for the majority of projects in the following years. Some charities, such as Barnardo's, NCH Action for Children and Crossroads, have dominated provision of specialist services for young carers, while other projects are managed by smaller local charities or voluntary

(Contd.)

(Box 3.3 Contd.)

agencies, and yet others are registered charities in their own right. An interesting development over more recent years has been the shift in location and emphasis, with more than a quarter of projects now located within carers' centres or other carer support groups. Many carers' centres now have designated workers to represent the interests of young carers and to work on their behalf.

Approximately one-tenth of specialist support services for young carers are now located within social services departments (Aldridge & Becker, 1998). In most cases this means that there is a worker with particular involvement in young carers' issues who may be responsible for the assessment of young carers' needs and those of their families under the appropriate legislation (see Chapter 2). While this move indicates the ser-iousness with which some local authorities are beginning to take young carers' issues, particularly in light of Department of Health findings that 'a high proportion of families interviewed reported little or no SSD contact (and no community care assessment) despite a long history of illness or disability' (DoH, 1996b: p. 13), we must also be wary that some families may avoid referral to statutory services for fear of punitive, invasive interventions, a fact borne out by the Department of Health's own research (1996b: p. 15).

Funding of projects

Although most projects are based within the voluntary sector, funding tends to come from statutory sources and projects experience the commonplace lack of financial security. In 1997, approximately 40% of projects received part of their core funding from joint finance (a mixture of social services and health authority funding), more than 40% from social services alone and slightly less than one-fifth from health authorities. Approximately one-fifth received some core funding from charities or voluntary organisations while only four projects received part of their core funding from education (Aldridge & Becker, 1998). In Britain, the introduction of the National Lottery has provided an additional potential source of funding, with nine projects receiving core funding and a further three receiving some additional funding in 1997. Corporate funding has been low, with only eight projects receiving some core funding and five in receipt of additional funding from this sector (Aldridge & Becker, 1998).

At the end of the 1996/1997 financial year, many young carers projects were reported to be facing financial crisis (Thompson, 1997). Of the 106 established projects in 1997, fewer than half considered future funding to be 'very likely' or 'likely', 12 considered it to be 'unlikely' or 'very unlikely' while more than 40 were unsure about the future (Aldridge & Becker, 1998). Problems with funding make project development difficult and workers are constantly facing the dilemma of whether to accept new referrals and try to support them when there may be no service available in the future. One of the major criticisms from project staff is that, in the light of such uncertainty, it is unacceptable to raise hopes which may not be fulfilled. A funding strategy which gives priority to young carers and

(Contd.)

(Box 3.3 Contd.)

their families as being in need of services and support, and which does not rely on the insecurity of short-term funding or the vagaries of a lottery, is essential if the needs of these families are to be met in a consistent and secure manner.

Project aims and objectives
All projects have evolved independently to meet the needs of local young carers, so each has its own aims. However, many projects do share objectives, the most common of these being awareness-raising of young carers' issues. This is viewed as a determining factor in recognising and meeting the needs of young carers among statutory and voluntary agencies, and it inevitably ties in with the second most common aim of developing or offering specific services to meet these needs. More than 70% of the projects identified by Aldridge and Becker (1998) cited the development of support services as one of their major aims. A quarter of projects included the aim of working in collaboration with or advising other agencies in order to meet needs. Approximately 10% of projects also aimed to influence policy and practice. These key objectives – raising awareness, working in partnership with other agencies, and direct service provision – are not only valued by young carers, but also by professionals (DoH, 1996b: p. 34).

Services provided
Although young carers projects have developed independently, the types of services they provide tend to be very similar. Most projects offer information and assistance to access other avenues of support. In this way workers are able to work together with families to help them access community care and other types of services which will benefit the care recipient, the young carer and the rest of the family. For example, in Sefton a member of the project advisory group was able to get charges for home care waived for families with young carers of school age (Mahon & Higgins, 1995); in Nottingham the project worker liaised with professionals and helped some families secure additional home care and special transport (Dearden & Becker, 1996); elsewhere project staff involve the whole family from the outset, as one project worker states:

> 'I feel that working with the child in isolation from the family is closing your eyes to the fact that if you change the situation of the young carers it's going to have implications for each and every member of that family.'

> (Quoted in Dearden & Becker, 1995a: p. 32)

Although working with families is an important aspect of the work of these projects, their primary focus is on supporting children as carers. In this respect most projects offer counselling, advocacy and befriending services specifically for young carers. Some of this counselling and befriending work is provided on an informal basis (someone to talk to, a confidante) although

(Contd.)

(Box 3.3 Contd.)

some projects provide or arrange more formal services where applicable. Advocacy is considered an essential service by many projects since many young carers – indeed many children – are unaware of their rights. Project workers can therefore work with them or act on their behalf to try and secure their rights under existing legislation. In working with and for the children in families, project workers have also been able to secure the rights and entitlements of other family members.

Around 80% of projects arrange leisure activities for young carers. Indeed, in many cases these are the services that young carers value most (see Mahon & Higgins, 1995; Dearden & Becker, 1996). The early maturation often associated with young caring, and the possible lack of time and space for leisure and extra-curricular activities, can make friendships difficult so that some young carers may have little in common with their peers (Bilsborrow, 1992; Aldridge & Becker, 1993a; Frank, 1995; Dearden & Becker, 1996). The leisure activities provided by projects serve the dual purpose of enabling children to have fun and allowing them to mix with others who share similar experiences.

Mixing with other young carers can serve to validate the young caring experience and reassure children that they are not alone. Although project workers stress the fact that young carers rarely sit around discussing their experiences or home lives, during interviews many young carers have said that it can be comforting to know that, among other young carers, there is no need to explain their circumstances and their feelings will be understood (Dearden & Becker, 1995a, 1996).

Family centres

We must not underestimate the challenges inherent in moving towards a whole family approach to meet the needs of young carers and their ill or disabled parents. Cannan and Warren (1997) argue that 'children's and family services need recasting in a community development framework' (what they term *social action*) and that social workers need to draw on this strand of their profession 'in order to share in the task of promoting child and family well-being' (p. 1).

Cannan and Warren emphasise the importance and value of family centres as a 'key mechanism of supporting families by helping them promote their children's welfare', particularly those centres which adopt a community development approach (Cannan & Warren, 1997: p. 7). Moreover, family centres, in their many forms, can help to prevent problems and monitor families, as Hardiker *et al.* (1991) suggest:

'Family centres may take many forms, from a primary developmental role to an institutional or even a residual one, providing supplementary care, teaching parents better parenting, monitoring children's progress and providing increased professional surveillance of vulnerable and disadvantaged families.'

(p. 355)

Evidence from the UK, USA and Europe suggests that neighbourhood family centres are an effective means of promoting family support (Cannan & Warren, 1997; Lloyd, 1997). Centres reach a large number of people, bridging the generations, encouraging 'user ownership' and self esteem, and contributing to local friendship networks. They also have a 'particular quality which cannot be replicated in the bureaucratic offices of social services departments' (Cannan & Warren, 1997: p. 8). Cannan and Warren believe that family centres 'offer a new paradigm for practice ... a model and a setting for integrated family support practice in the context of child focused provision' (1997: p. 10).

Given the strategic importance of family centres in the matrix of service provisions that exist to meet the needs of local families, there is undoubtedly scope for family centre approaches and practices to be extended to meet some of the needs of young carers and their families. As they stand, few family centres provide this specific support, although many will already be in contact with ill and disabled people and their families. The primary focus of young carers projects, as we have seen, has been traditionally on the child within the context of their family and caring life. Warren (1997) suggests that young carers projects can be an important vehicle on a 'journey of empowerment' for children and, where they provide wider family support, for parents as well. There seems considerable scope, therefore, for family centre practices to be adopted more extensively by young carers projects, thus promoting the inclusion and participation of parents as well as young carers. Conversely, family centres themselves may wish to be more open to young carers and their families by being explicit in what they have to offer.

For those geographical areas without a young carers project family centres could become a possible focus for work with young carers and their families. Indeed it is conceivable that family centres may in due course take over some of this work from projects (particularly those with precarious funding arrangements), or that young carers projects could become integrated into neighbourhood family centres in the longer term. Whatever the final relationship between young carers projects and neighbourhood family centres there is a clear need for greater flexibility on the part of both organisations to cater for young carers and their families. Local experiments of joint working or integration would be a valuable way to proceed, with monitoring and evaluation leading to the dissemination of models of good practice.

Information and advice

A significant factor in implementing successful and appropriate support services to young carers and their families is the provision of information. Much of the research on young carers has emphasised that families have urgent needs for a range of information on such issues as domestic and social support, benefits, medical assistance and voluntary help. Information services should be both family orientated and specific to individuals.

Information provision should also therefore be child-centred, as children are all too often left out of the information equation (see Aldridge & Becker, 1993a). It is possible that providing information to children about services and medical conditions could prevent their isolation and seclusion and may, to some extent, prevent them from either continuing to care unaided or undertaking extensive and intensive caring roles in the first place. Aldridge and Becker (1993a) found that children were often woefully uninformed, not only about where to go for help or support for themselves and their families but also about the medical condition they were helping to manage. In most cases the children knew so little about their parent's medical condition that they had invented their own versions of diagnosis, prognosis and the possible consequences in respect of their own health. Recent evidence suggests that lack of information is still a major factor in relation to the needs of young carers and their families: 'Families interviewed had had considerable difficulty in obtaining information about diagnoses and likely progression of illness or disability ... and in finding out about sources of support' (DoH, 1996b: p. 17).

Information provision may also be helpful in terms of identification procedures, in that if young carers and their families are aware of the caring choices available to them and know how to access appropriate services then they may also be more assertive in presenting their needs to empathic and responsive professionals. Thus, information should be a two-way process between families and welfare professionals. The latter need access to a body of information in order to provide families with the support they need. Aldridge and Becker (1997) have argued that it would be profitable if families were informed by welfare agencies about some of the issues surrounding young caring, for example when and how it can occur and how dependence on children for caring could be avoided. The authors have further argued that although welfare professionals cannot transform themselves into what they term 'virtuoso informants', it is not unreasonable to expect workers to be able to offer either some form of personal assistance in relation to information provision, or to refer families to alternative information sources if the workers do not have the answers to questions themselves: 'Over compensation in this respect would be preferable to a situation where nominal or partial advice is offered leaving families only further confused' (Aldridge & Becker, 1997: p. 12). Thus, as the Department of Health has argued, 'reliable information – for families and for professionals – is essential' (1996b: p. 17).

The Department of Health's recommendations in this respect are for joint training between children's and adult services and information that is aimed at young carers and their families in terms of health, 'community care processes and about service options', as well as the possibility of developing a management information database about young carers and families with illness or disability.

The roles and responsibilities of welfare professionals

The provision of appropriate services to young carers and their families involves a number of professional strategies. In the first instance, welfare professionals should be identifying young carers, which requires ongoing strategies to raise awareness, the introduction of training and development programmes, multi-agency support, co-ordination of services to improve inter-agency communication and facilitate easy access to support services, and the ongoing monitoring and review of cases. Professionals should assist families to consider the roles of family members and the responsibilities they have towards each other. They should also help families make decisions and plans about future care arrangements which are not to the detriment of children.

Awareness-raising and identification

In some respects, by the very emergence of young caring as a subject for research and debate, and its subsequent development both theoretically and practically, strategies to raise the profile of young carers are ongoing. The recent focus on young carers by academics and policy makers alike has resulted in awareness of the issue being raised both publicly and professionally. Organisations such as the Carers National Association, Crossroads and Barnardo's have played their part in a nationwide awareness-raising campaign which has been closely monitored by an attentive national media.

On a practical level the growing interest in young carers' issues has not only emphasised the need for support services and generated public interest, but more significantly it has helped to change policy. Previously the specific needs of child carers were embraced neither by the NHS and Community Care Act nor the Children Act. However, as a result of research strategies and extensive campaigning young carers have been included in the Carers (Recognition and Services) Act which was implemented in April 1996 and their needs are now often met under the Children Act provision for children in need (see Chapter 2).

A wide range of support services have since been set up across the country, from respite care schemes to befriending projects (see Dearden & Becker, 1995b). Furthermore the young carers debate has alerted many professionals both to the reality of the young caring experience and the *potential* for it. The increasing focus on young carers' issues has served to highlight to the child welfare services the many circumstances in which young caring is founded and maintained.

However, it is still crucial that, through training programmes, professionals are made aware of the multifarious circumstances in which young caring can be found. A crucial 'trigger' would be the presence of parental illness/disability, although professionals should not presume young caring is established or is an inevitable outcome of parental impairment in families. Further indications of young caring may be evident in children's behavioural responses – emotional stress, difficulties at school, health problems etc. – and so a range of key health or education professionals may be required to identify the presence of young caring in families and direct these families to appropriate services. The Department of Health suggests that it is important to: 'Develop triggers to help professionals in all agencies recognise family circumstances where young caring might occur [and] establish protocols to ensure that, regardless of initial contact – health, education or social services – families with young carers will be routed appropriately for services' (DoH, 1996b: p. 15).

Multi-agency support and co-ordinated services

As Fuller (1989) has argued, although there may be a number of different agencies involved with a single client, and a client's problems may be interlinked, this should not be an obstacle to a co-ordinated approach using multi-agency support procedures. In order to assist young carers and their families there has to be a commitment to such multi-agency support at all levels. The Department of Health has argued that young carers should be identified in Children's Services Plans and Community Care Plans 'which should be cross-referenced' (1996b: p. 16). Furthermore, an Amendment to the Children Act 1989 means that 'Guidance on children's services planning [LAC(96)10] calls for services for young carers to be closely co-ordinated with community care services for parents who are disabled or mentally ill' (DoH, 1996b: p. 16). In addition, the Department of Health stresses that the need for a family approach should be secured at all levels and across agencies.

Evidence from the young carers literature has suggested that services for young carers and their disabled parents are rarely co-ordinated. Aldridge and Becker (1994) found, for example, that some families had access to a range of services but individual organisations were frequently unaware of any other professional intervention in these families' lives. Furthermore, the services that were provided often were not what families had asked for or said they needed. To compound these problems, most welfare professionals had overlooked both the presence and the role of the child in each case. Clearly, what young carers and their families need are support services that signal cross-referencing and free-flowing communication channels between agencies. Furthermore, services should be adaptable, compatible, and based on what families say they need rather than what professionals feel they can offer (given available resources) or think would be best. The Department of Health suggests that services should also span district or divisional boundaries and that this should be consistent regardless of family migration.

Monitoring of cases

The disability rights challenge to the work on young carers has suggested that one of the negative consequences of the debate has been that welfare professionals now have their 'young carers spectacles on' (Parker & Olsen, 1995: p. 70) when responding to families' needs. However, in order to prevent the further neglect of young carers and to create scenarios where young carers are included in policy decisions and service plans, it is a necessary facet of positive intervention that welfare professionals are aware of the 'triggers' that signal the presence of young carers in vulnerable families. Furthermore, it is imperative that the *continued* vigilance and responsiveness of professionals is reinforced and maintained in order to prevent future crises in these families.

Professional intervention should not end at the point of service delivery to families. Aldridge and Becker (1997) have argued that some form of 'beneficent observation' or ongoing assessment should be carried out by those professionals involved with vulnerable families whose circumstances may be either uncertain, in transition or even in crisis (when children might be called on to care if support services have failed or new and different needs have arisen).

Thus, professionals should engage in the ongoing responsibility of assessment, monitoring and evaluation and improve their communication with other professionals who may also have further involvement with these families. It is important that young carers and their families do not become lost in an over-pressurised system that means professionals cannot undertake review and reassessment procedures. The Department of Health has called for a programme of monitoring and review so that 'the future and changing needs of young carers and their families are not forgotten' (DoH, 1996b: p. 30).

Monitoring families for signs of crisis or the arrival of new or different needs does not have to rely simply on individual responses and family centres could have a key role to play in this respect.

Assisting with family decision-making and care planning

How can ill or disabled parents and young carers make family-based decisions and plan for their future while ensuring the needs, safety and welfare of all family members? Families may sometimes need professional assistance to make decisions about caring and other arrangements in such a way that these decisions do not work against the interests (or rights) of other family members, particularly the children.

The family group conference (FGC) offers a potentially valuable way for parents, young carers and wider kinship groups to meet in a formal manner to consider a range of issues and make decisions about caring arrangements, both familial and professional. The emphasis is on families working together to decide explicitly what must be done and by whom, rather than professionals making these decisions on the family's behalf.

Family group conferences originated in New Zealand and were developed initially as a means of meeting the needs of Maori children and families: 'They introduced a model for decision making in child care and protection that was unique in Western jurisdictions' (Tunnard, 1997: p. 165). Their success led to their inclusion in primary legislation and to their use for all families and in all areas of children and family work in that country. In the UK, the model is currently being piloted in a number of settings, including family and youth justice work, and is being carefully evaluated by a research team. Consequently, there is a growing body of literature on the use and application of FGCs (see for example Marsh & Crow, 1997).

FGCs could be a useful strategy for improving decision-making within families where children are engaged in caring roles, and for professionals working in partnership with families. Tunnard asserts that three crucial elements are necessary for the term 'family group conference' to be appropriate. First, the 'family' is interpreted widely to include relatives, friends and other significant people; second, the family must always have the opportunity to plan in private; and third, the family's plan must always be accepted by professionals unless the plan places the child at risk of significant harm (Tunnard, 1997: p. 164). The mechanisms for how such conferences should be organised and run are outlined in depth in the literature on FGCs and it is inappropriate to recount the detail here (see for example Marsh & Crow, 1997; Tunnard, 1997: pp. 164–5). What is important for our purposes is the extent to which FGCs might be used by parents and young carers to make decisions and plan for their joint future, and to make demands on professionals to assist in the achievement of these plans. Involvement in this process could be profoundly empowering for parents and young carers: 'Empowerment is about agencies planning services from a user perspective, and then working in partnership with users to meet their defined needs and preferred solutions' (Tunnard, 1997: p. 180).

Where professionals are involved with young carers and their families, particularly with those young carers defined as 'in need' under the Children Act, FGCs should be considered as a strategic way forward for decision-making and planning. They provide an opportunity for parents and young carers to negotiate explicitly the roles and responsibilities that they have towards each other, and to decide what they both require of professionals from a range of settings, including social services, health, education and so on. Moreover, professionals are required to agree the plan and negotiate the resources necessary to achieve its aims, unless the plan places a level of caring and other responsibilities on the child which are likely to impair their health or development or place them at risk of significant harm.

Chapter 5 considers these issues in more detail. Chapter 4 now considers young caring as a British *and* international phenomenon.

Chapter 4
Young Carers: A Cross-national Perspective

Introduction

In this chapter, some of the implications of cross-national demographic changes and trends for informal care-givers, particularly young carers and their families, are examined. The focus is predominantly European (including Britain) and Australian because of the availability of information and data, although reference is made to other countries where there are relevant developments, including the United States and Israel. In particular, we are concerned to assess the extent to which the balance between state provision and family support, and the nature of the welfare 'mix' in a particular country, affects the experiences of and responses to young carers and their families. Despite almost global concerns over the ageing of the population, the squeeze on resources, and the pressure on family members to care for each other, each country has different ways of dealing with these patterns of change.

Trends

Throughout the world populations are ageing. This trend is caused by a number of factors, including the growth in the *proportion* of people aged over 65; the increase in *absolute* numbers of older people; and the improvement of life expectancy at birth (Hugman, 1994). In the European Union (EU), it is estimated that by 2025 there will be an increase of 38 million people (almost 50%) aged 60 and over. This will bring the total number of pensioners to about 114 million, nearly a third of the EU population. In the United States, by 2030, the proportion of people aged 65 and over will rise from 12% to more than 18% of the population. The proportion of 'very elderly' (those aged 75 and over) will increase by 71% within the next decade alone (Beach, 1994: p. 12).

Other trends are also significantly changing the demographic profile of nations. Disabled people are the largest minority in the world, totalling more than 500 million people, of whom two thirds live in developing countries (Degener, 1995). In the EU it is estimated that there are about 30 million people (approximately 10% of the population) who currently suffer from some kind of long-term physical or mental disability (Glendinning & McLaughlin, 1993).

The ratio of older dependants to people of working age is also increasing across the developed world. In Europe, by 2025, the number of young people under 20 years of age will fall by 9.5 million, or 11% (Ruxton, 1996). In the UK there will be a concurrent increase of 44% in the population aged over 60, combined with a 2.8% *decline* in the working population and an 8.2% *drop* in the under 20s. The trend is similar throughout most of Europe, and raises some potential difficulties for all European welfare states, namely who will pay or care for vulnerable groups (Millar & Warman, 1996).

These problems are potentially exacerbated by other changes taking place across Europe and elsewhere. Everywhere family size is declining and the family unit has been destabilised (Hantrais, 1992a; Monnier & Guibert-Lantoine, 1993). There has been a drop in fertility rates across Europe, and large families have become an exception. Extramarital cohabitation rates and the proportion of births outside marriage are increasing, as is lone parenthood, and the number of separations, divorces and recomposed families (Meulders-Klein & Théry, 1993).

Since the 1980s, these new family patterns have been accompanied by another cross-national trend: the de-institutionalisation of caring, or 'care in the community'. For example, in the 1970s, France pursued a policy designed to encourage disabled and elderly people to remain in their own homes (Laroque, 1985). In 1993, an allowance was introduced to support independent living for disabled adults. In the 1980s, Sweden started to close down institutions for older people and those with mental health problems, and in 1993 local authorities were made responsible for paying a carer chosen by the disabled person. In Britain, after a long history of de-institutionalisation of care, dating back to the 1950s in the case of mental health problems, and in line with the privatisation of public sector services, the National Health Service (NHS) and Community Care Act 1990 confirmed the responsibility of local authority social services departments for ensuring the care of elderly and disabled people as far as possible within their own homes (see Chapter 2 for a full discussion of the policy context). In Germany in 1995, in a social context which stresses the individual responsibility of households, compulsory insurance was introduced against the costs of long-term care.

The aim of these different measures has been to enable chronically ill people, those with mental health problems, and people with physical or learning disabilities to remain in their own home instead of being admitted to an institution. This form of privatisation of care has been justified both on economic and social grounds. All governments are looking for ways of cutting public spending and the cost of care in the home is thought to be lower than in an institution. It is generally believed that elderly and disabled people prefer to remain in their own homes surrounded by friends and relatives (Laroque, 1985), while older children tend to feel they have failed socially if they allow a sick or elderly person to be taken into an institution (Jani-Le Bris, 1993).

To varying degrees throughout Europe and the developed world, state support schemes for elderly and disabled people are coming under pressure as rising numbers of citizens require pensions, health and social care. As the pension age is raised in some countries, including Britain where the pensionable age for men and women has been equalised, and as the proportion of younger people available to provide family care decreases, there will be greater pressure on family members to begin or continue to provide care, and greater pressure on people to combine paid employment with care-giving (Berry-Lound & Marsh, 1996; George & Taylor-Gooby, 1996).

Moreover, there may be more pressure on children to take on caring roles within the family, either as the sole carer or helping the main carer, perhaps a parent. Figures from the European Community Household Panel survey indicate that, in 1994, 16 million children under the age of 16 (24% of all children in Europe) live in households with one person 'hampered in daily activities by any chronic physical or mental health problem, illness or disability'. In the UK, the figure is 2.8 million, equivalent to 23% of all children (Eurostat, 1997). It is impossible to estimate the proportion of children who have no caring responsibilities or those that will take on some caring tasks. Meanwhile, in the United States, data show that while 75% of informal carers are female (with an average age of 46), almost one third of these women have children at home who are under 12 years of age, and 23% have a child aged 12 to 17 living with them (Beach, 1997: p. 234). Again, it is impossible to estimate what proportion of these children help their mother to provide care within the family.

The pressure on European state welfare systems will be reinforced by the convergence criteria for the EU's intended economic and monetary union, which stresses the need to avoid excessive public sector spending deficits. Consequently, while there is no intention of harmonising social policies across Europe, there is a clear convergence towards the development of social care systems that place less emphasis on state agencies as *providers* of care and more importance on 'informal' sector care provision (family, friends and the voluntary/charitable sector). The development of the private (for profit) sector is also growing. This is also the case in other developed countries, for example Australia and New Zealand. Most of these countries' welfare systems are characterised by a mixed economy, although the balance between the 'mix' varies significantly between different countries, depending on tradition, politics and economic factors (Munday & Ely, 1996; Hantrais, 1995).

Carers in Europe

A report by the Foundation for the Improvement of Living and Working Conditions, analysing the situation of carers in the European Union at the end of the 1980s, confirmed that throughout Europe the family is the foundation of care for older and disabled people, almost irrespective of the country's family, social and socio-political structures (Jani-Le Bris, 1993). However, in most countries, little recognition is given to the contribution of family carers, nor is there much support for them from statutory authorities: 'Virtually all social policies count on, or entirely depend on the family – yet few Member States have taken any practical steps to provide that primary pillar with any real support' (Jani-Le Bris, 1993: p. 10). This is despite the knowledge that care-giving in all countries can have adverse effects on the physical, mental, social and moral well-being of the individuals concerned.

Information on the characteristics of carers across Europe is incomplete because so many countries do not collect much data on them. Britain leads the way in terms of information and knowledge of family carers and specific policy responses geared towards meeting some of their needs. Britain was the first, for example, to have a national association to promote the needs of carers and lobby on their behalf, and it was one of the first countries to generate coherent research on carers, much of which came initially from feminist writers. Moreover, Britain is one of the few countries which compiles national statistics on carers (see for example OPCS, 1992).

Despite the lack of comparative data, Jani-Le Bris (1993) has been able to identify some characteristics which are common to carers across national boundaries. For example, she discovered that most carers across Europe are women – wives, daughters and daughters-in-law, in that hierarchy. Moreover, carers rarely have any genuine 'choice' as to whether or not to provide care. Most are drawn into caring through one of two routes: either through a 'slow creeping process' or following a sudden incident, motivated by a sense of 'duty' prevailing even where there is little attachment or affection to the 'recipient of care'. Finally, she discovered that carers throughout the EU have an urgent need for support – practical, material, emotional and social – which is exacerbated by a lack of co-ordination in social welfare services, with carers falling through the gaps in service provision (Jani-Le Bris, 1993).

Defining family obligations and family policy in Europe

The experiences of carers, why they are drawn into caring and why they remain as carers, will in part be determined by the availability of support services and cash payments for them and the people for whom they care. Consequently, it is important to understand the nature of the welfare mix in different countries (for example, the role of the state compared with the role of the private and voluntary sectors). However, the most significant factor is the social and legal expectations on family members to provide or pay for the care of dependent family members. It is therefore important to get some sense of the welfare mix within countries if we are to understand why carers care.

A number of attempts have been made to categorise the family policies that have been formulated and implemented in different countries over the post-war period. One of the earliest attempts by Kamerman and Kahn (1978) distinguished between countries with explicit and implicit family policies. Explicit and global policies, according to these two authors, were characteristic of France, the former Czechoslovakia, Hungary and the Scandinavian countries, except for Denmark. Some countries were said to have an explicit but less specific family policy, namely Denmark, Germany, Austria, Poland and Finland. The same authors classified the United Kingdom, Canada, Israel and the United States as countries that rejected the idea of state intervention in family life.

More recently in Britain, Millar and Warman (1996), working in collaboration with a network of researchers from 15 other western European countries, examined how the balance between state provision and family support is defined in law and policy across Europe. In terms of informal care-giving, Millar and Warman's analysis of the structures and policies within each country enabled them to divide the countries into four groups. In each group common approaches to defining the extent and range of family obligations towards older or disabled relatives were identified. These groups ranged from those with legally defined family obligations to care for dependent relatives or pay for their care, to those countries with individual entitlement and clearly defined state responsibilities, with far less reliance on family provision of care.

Extended family (Italy, Spain and Portugal)

In this group there are legal obligations between extended family members to provide financial support for each other. The state itself has little responsibility for supporting individuals. Individuals who need assistance with care tasks or long-term care would have to pay for it. Those without the means turn to family members who are obliged to pay for the care or provide the support themselves.

Parents and children (Austria, Belgium, France, Germany, Greece and Luxembourg)

Civil codes formally give adult children maintenance responsibilities towards their parents. Adult children are defined as 'liable relatives' and they can be asked to pay for the care of parents. Most of these countries also have legislation which allows the state the power to reclaim social assistance benefits from adult children.

In Austria and Germany adult children have, in theory, financial obligations to pay for the care needs of their parents but recent policy has moved so as not to enforce payment but to require individuals in employment to take out care insurance.

No clear state responsibility (Ireland and the UK)

Family members have no formal, legal obligations to provide or pay for the care of older people or disabled adults, but the responsibilities of the state are also not clearly defined. However, local regulations in the UK have required family members in some circumstances to make financial contributions towards the care of their elderly parents.

Clear state responsibility (Denmark, Finland, The Netherlands, Norway and Sweden)

State obligations to adults with care needs are made explicit and it is the individual to whom support is directed. In practice, the costs of domiciliary care, or even long-term care, which cannot be met by an individual will be paid through a government/local authority scheme. In many of these countries there is legislation giving authorities explicit duties to maintain vulnerable people in their own homes within the community. However, irrespective of these clearly defined state responsibilities, family members in these countries still take on caring roles (Millar & Warman, 1996).

Payments for care

Millar and Warman (1996) also examined 'payments for care' in different countries, and whether these went to care-givers, care-receivers, or to both. Some countries, particularly Sweden and Norway, allow family members to be formally employed by a local authority to provide day-to-day care to other family members, with no time limits. Those countries where extended family members are legally obliged to provide care are least likely to have payment schemes (often, the obligations of families to care for each other are so deep-rooted that they do not need to be encouraged by payments).

Many developed countries have, or are introducing, some kind of financial support for carers alongside the provision of care services to people with long-term care needs. The rationale for this has been along the lines that financial support for family carers might mitigate reductions in the availability of 'able-bodied' family members who could provide informal care. Additionally, these payments may also sustain informal care relationships and prevent caring breakdowns and costly admissions to residential care for the person with care needs.

Glendinning and McLaughlin's (1993) study of payment schemes in seven European countries (including Britain) provides more details of such schemes and raises key issues as to whether carers should be paid at all (and if so why, how, and how much). In most European countries payments for care are either decided at central government level and implemented by local and regional organisations, or are embedded entirely within local social welfare services. In these latter schemes, the overall budget, the criteria employed in deciding who should get a cash allowance, and the amount they should receive are all decided at local level. Such decisions usually involve welfare professionals making judgements and using their discretion. A major consequence of this is the wide local variations that exist in payments to carers *within* and *between* countries. Carers in identical situations in one country find themselves receiving different levels of allowances – or indeed no payment at all. Territorial inequity is a growing political issue. By contrast, the UK invalid care allowance for carers is provided as a right – an entitlement provided through the national social security system. However, the benefit is criticised by Glendinning and McLaughlin (1993) as being largely ineffective (it is too low and does not reach many in most need).

Glendinning and McLaughlin's research indicates that payment schemes to carers do not increase the overall level of informal care-giving. However, payments may help to sustain the care-giving relationship for longer than would otherwise have been the case and this might help to lower rates of admission to residential care. On the whole it also appears that payment schemes act as substitutes for domiciliary services rather than as complements to them. Because conventional services are so useful for carers, even at relatively low levels, authorities should be wary of looking to substitute these with cash support. However, as far as the UK is concerned, there is scope to improve the current system. This could be done by increasing the rate of invalid care allowance towards the level of care allowances elsewhere in Europe so that it provides more effective income maintenance for carers, and by introducing employment measures to facilitate the combination of paid work and informal care-giving.

The balance between state and family

Both Millar and Warman (1996) and Glendinning and McLaughlin (1993) demonstrate how different countries have a different balance between state provision (in services and cash) and family support. While the UK has more direct state provision for carers than some other countries (most notably Italy, Portugal and Spain, but also Austria and Greece), carers' rights in the UK are not as far-reaching as in countries such as Sweden, Denmark and Norway. Millar and Warman conclude that there are two extremes of approach. In southern Europe (Italy, Greece, Spain and Portugal) family members are required by law to provide support and state provision is thus low and discretionary. Carers are rarely paid or compensated and cannot easily opt out of their care obligations. Autonomy or independence from family (for care-givers or care-receivers) is not an objective of policy nor are there clear state entitlements to support for either group.

By contrast, in Scandinavian countries, independence is a goal of policy and social care is more likely to be an individual right, albeit mediated by the discretionary judgements of welfare professionals. Levels of service provision are high and family members can, if they wish, opt out of providing day-to-day care. There is a strong element of choice about taking on the role of carer which is absent in the southern European countries (Millar & Warman, 1996).

Clearly, the boundary between family and state responsibilities for dependent adults reflects the different notions of family obligations which are evident across Europe. From this, it is clear that some people with physical or mental impairments, older people, etc., will be able to receive considerable support (and cash) from the state, as will some family carers. This is particularly so for those carers and their dependants living in Scandinavian countries, where independence and autonomy, for care-receivers and care-givers, are goals of social policy. The UK occupies a position somewhere between the two extremes of those countries where there are legal obligations for extended or nuclear family members to care for each other, or where there are clear state responsibilities to provide care and where families can 'opt out' of this role.

However, despite the differing boundaries between state and family responsibility which exist in different countries, the evidence suggests that the critical contribution and role of informal care-givers, throughout the European Union, is still not acknowledged sufficiently, nor have carers' needs been explicitly addressed by most Member States, irrespective of the boundary between state provision and family support, or the particular 'welfare mix' within that country. Jani-Le Bris (1993) outlines twenty nine policy recommendations intended to raise the profile of carers across the EU and to help develop services which will 'care for the carers'. They are 'based on the idea that choice must be a basic principle guaranteed to family carers' (p. 129). Box 4.1 provides a summary of some of Jani-Le Bris' main recommendations.

Young carers in Europe

Nowhere is the neglect of informal care-givers more evident than in the case of young carers. Young carers experience a 'double jeopardy'

Box 4.1 A summary of the key recommendations for improving the lives of carers from the European Foundation for the Improvement of Living and Working Conditions

Countries must:

- ensure that the specific needs and role of the family in caring are recognised and made the object of social and political measures which improve the carer's quality of life on an everyday basis
- establish social policies for the elderly which include measures for carers
- promote, create or strengthen all forms of respite care
- ensure financial compensation and assistance is available to carers and their families
- provide sickness and pension coverage for carers in connection with disability and old age
- encourage and support the creation of associations of carers, both local and national, and encourage the development of support groups for carers
- introduce a series of specific measures designed for carers to help them remain in paid employment
- promote opportunities for training carers and for providing them with information
- include instruction on the specific problems of carers within professional training programmes to social workers, doctors etc.
- create, extend or restructure home-based services to benefit users and carers
- promote and ensure the development of further social research about family carers.

Source: Jani-Le Bris (1993: pp. 129–147)

because of their status as children and as carers. It is clear that most European countries (and elsewhere) have failed to collect adequate statistics on informal care-givers (Jani-Le Bris, 1993), and the same is true of their data collection relating to children: 'children receive minimal coverage in EU statistics' (Ruxton, 1996: p. 17). The information regarding the position of children *within families* is particularly limited. Ruxton (1996: p. 67), for example, highlights the problems across Europe of gaining transnational information on even basic issues, such as the age distribution of children within families and the implications and outcomes for children living in different family settings and at different income levels. It is not surprising therefore that there are no official data whatsoever on young carers in Europe.

One of the few available comparative studies to date is that conducted by Becker and colleagues (Becker, 1995b). Their exploratory study in France, Sweden and Germany developed and complemented Aldridge and Becker's earlier research conducted in England (Chapter 1; also see Aldridge & Becker, 1993a, 1994). One of the aims of this cross-national approach was to examine the reactions to young carers in different policy environments (Becker, 1995a). With this objective in mind, a number of hypotheses were used. First, it might be anticipated that countries with an explicit interventionist state role and relatively coherent family policy would be able to avert situations where young children are having to look after a sick or disabled parent, by providing non-stigmatising help and support. Second, countries with a universalist welfare system should be able to provide more support than those where social protection is dependent on insurance-based social security centred on the working population. Finally, countries with a less explicit family policy, particularly where there is an insurance-based welfare system, or where care is being privatised and public spending is being severely curtailed, might be expected to make little if any public provision for young carers, the more so when voluntary services are widely accepted as an addition to or substitute for state provision (Hantrais & Becker, 1995; Davis Smith, 1993).

As we have seen, France, Sweden, Germany and Great Britain have different boundaries between state provision and family support (Millar & Warman, 1996), and represent different categories of family policy (Hantrais, 1995; Hantrais & Becker, 1995). Sweden (Pauti, 1992) and France (Schultheis, 1991) share a long tradition of legitimised state intervention in family life based on a broad social consensus, even if their family policy objectives differ. In France, family policy has familial origins (Lenoir, 1991) and falls into Millar and Warman's category of 'parents and children', where civil codes formally confer on adult children maintenance responsibilities towards their parents. Swedish family policy is founded on the ideology of equality and social justice (Pauti, 1992) and, in Millar and Warman's classification, it is defined as one of those countries where state obligations to people with care needs are explicit and interventionist. Germany holds an intermediate position which derives from a very strong normative conception of the legitimate conjugal family that leaves little room for deviation (Schultheis, 1992; Lefranc, 1994). Britain belongs to the group of countries where there is no clear state responsibility (Millar & Warman, 1996) and where state intervention in families has long been rejected on the grounds that family life is a private affair (Schultheis, 1990), except if children are at risk (Hantrais, 1992b, 1994).

Social attitudes concerning the place of children in society are also likely to be important factors determining reactions to young carers in different societal contexts: Swedish social policy, for example, is known to give priority to equality issues and the well-being of children for reasons of social justice; French policy focuses attention on families as a key social institution and of fundamental social value, while also paying attention to measures enabling couples to combine work and family life; German policy gives priority to the legitimate couple and to the primary role of mothers in the home; and British social policy attaches importance both to respect for privacy and the protection of children at risk (Hantrais & Becker, 1995: p. 80).

Defining young carers in different national contexts

Governments in Britain have been reluctant to intervene directly in the private lives of families except when children are in danger, and in the 1950s Britain was among the first countries in western Europe to implement the de-institutionalisation of caring (Ramon, 1987) and to formulate supportive policies to assist carers (Jani-Le Bris, 1993). While the feminist literature, particularly in Britain, was quick to recognise that community care policies were detrimental to women and demanded that the role of carer should be re-conceptualised (Ungerson, 1990), the situation of young carers remained invisible in the absence of a lobby to represent their interests. While the burden placed on women was considered unacceptable in a context where, despite their increasing participation in economic activity, they still bore the major responsibility for child care, household tasks and caring for elderly people, the responsibilities young carers faced were only beginning to be examined during the late 1980s.

Britain was one of the first countries where researchers and others took an interest in young carers. A national organisation (the Carers National Association) was set up to address the problem, while an academic body (the Young Carers Research Group at Loughborough University) was established to research national and cross-national issues concerned with child carers.

Young carers are not easy to identify, either in Britain or elsewhere, because in most countries they are not an officially recognised welfare category. The NHS and Community Care Act 1990 in Britain does not, for example, make any reference to children who care, although the Carers (Recognition and Services) Act 1995 does include young carers in its province and the Children Act 1989 has proven useful in meeting the needs of some young carers who are defined as 'children in need' (see Chapter 2). Moreover, there are no precise figures available on the number of young carers in Britain, although there are statistics available on the characteristics of young carers (Dearden & Becker, 1995a, 1998).

Brittain's (1995) exploratory study of young carers in France, as part of a collaboration between a number of researchers examining the situation in France, Sweden and Germany (Becker, 1995b), shows that young carers have not been a focus of attention for researchers, despite earlier provision in the French Social Security Code for an allowance to be paid to young girls who look after younger siblings and who undertake household duties where a parent is unable to do so. In France in 1989, more than 1200 girls aged between 17 and 20 were in receipt of the allowance, compared with some 4000 in 1980. At an official level, therefore, the state recognised that young girls could be called upon to forego their education in order to perform caring work, but at the same time, under civil and penal law, legislation for the protection of young children empowers the state to intervene to prevent children from being harmed by circumstances which may adversely affect their physical or mental well-being. Brittain reports that French policy makers claim not to be aware of the problem of young carers and do not consider it to be an issue worthy of further research. He suggests that at the time there were no data on the number of young carers at national level, and none of the national surveys made it possible to extrapolate how many children are performing caring tasks. Brittain accessed young carers in France mainly through voluntary, non-governmental organisations such as the Association Huntington de France, Association France Alzheimer et Troubles Apparentés and Association pour la Recherche sur la Sclérose en Plaques. Members of these organisations and psychiatric social workers were aware of the existence of young carers, but they were often reluctant to identify them for deontological reasons and because they believed that it would be detrimental to the children concerned if they were to be interviewed.

Gould's (1995) study of young carers in Sweden found that no previous research had been conducted on children as informal carers and no national data were available. He accessed young carers through the co-operation of two social services departments. In Sweden, the general view among policy makers and professionals is that the welfare system is so effective that the family of a sick or disabled person would not hesitate to request help and would be certain to receive it. Anyone suffering from a long-term illness or disability requiring home care has a legal right to the services of a personal carer. While no stigma is attached to seeking help in cases of physical disability, the situation is different in the case of mental ill-health, drug or alcohol misuse, where children are more likely to be removed from a family environment which is considered unsuitable for their upbringing (Gould, 1995; Hantrais & Becker, 1995).

In Germany, official documents and research literature rarely mention young carers, who are classified within the general category of relatives with caring responsibilities; there are about 2500 under-18s who are counted as carers looking after someone in need of regular attention. However, this number is likely to be far higher. Dietz and Clasen (1995) suggest that there may be as many as 72 000 children who take major responsibilities for caring, with tens of thousands more who share the care with others.

The case studies presented by Brittain (1995), Gould (1995) and Dietz and Clasen (1995) show that young carers are involved in a similar range of roles and responsibilities in France, Sweden and Germany. These findings are almost identical to those from qualitative and quantitative studies in Britain (Aldridge & Becker, 1993a; Dearden &

Becker, 1995a) and in Australia (Price, 1996). Box 4.2 provides brief quotations from young carers in these five countries to illustrate some of their circumstances and experiences.

Box 4.2   Young carers in Europe and Australia speak out

'When I think about all those years I cared for my dad, it makes me angry, not because I had to care for him – I *wanted* to care for him – but because I was left alone to cope with his illness for so long. I wasn't just doing ordinary tasks like other kids might do around the house. I was having to cook for him, beg for money and food parcels so I could feed him, take him to the toilet, clean him up when he couldn't get to the toilet – because he couldn't get up the stairs towards the end. No one should have to see their parents like that, when they lose all their bodily functions. I loved my dad and I couldn't bear to see him losing his dignity – getting more ill before my eyes ... It's too late for me now. My dad died and I'm no longer a 'young carer', but for all those other kids out there who are in the same situation I was, then something should be done to help them. Not take them away from their mum or dad, but to help them care without worrying, without being frightened.'

Jimmy, aged 16, who cared for his dying father, Great Britain

'I had to push dad in his wheelchair in the street because mum was too embarrassed to do it. Neither of them know how I felt during that time ... I have told you [the researcher] a lot of things about my relationship with my father that neither he nor my mother know ... Caring for my father destroyed my teenage years. In that situation there is no such thing as respite.'

Sabine, now an adult, who cared during her childhood for her father, France

'I tried and tried but it all became too much. Every time she would scream at me. In the end I gave up. I was able to say to myself that I wasn't obliged to support her. I don't have to have a mother. I don't have to suffer the guilt of having to be responsible for her.'

Monica, aged 20, who cared during her childhood for her mother who had mental health problems, Sweden

'I had to lift her, give her the medicine, take her to the toilet and so on. Later, when she was completely bed-bound I received help from my mother. Both of us made the beds and showered her together. My mother was completely overworked at the time. She couldn't cope any more ... Granny was embarrassed in front of me. She was ashamed, for example, to be washed by me – but less so by my mother. Later, however, she did not even notice any longer who it was who washed her.'

Michaela, aged 15, who cared for her grandmother, Germany

(Contd.)

(Box 4.2 Contd.)

'In March 1969, my mother turned 18 years old. It was a great year until she contracted a very bad episode of the measles. Mum never fully recovered. She stayed very weak and it was a real effort for her to walk. She was very frightened about what was happening to her and the doctor's didn't know what was wrong... Dad left mum when she was pregnant with me, so mum had me alone. It nearly killed mum having me. She was in hospital for 12 months afterwards and was paralysed from the neck down. Now, I'm 17 years old and I care for her. Mum was recently in hospital and she came home with a tracheostomy tube. I have been caring for mum for three years now. I left school at the age of 15 years. She has a gastrostomy tube and is unable to walk without help or on some bad days, using a wheelchair. She needs help on the toilet, in the shower, brushing her hair and teeth etc. I'm not normal. I don't go many places. I don't go to school. My life is very different and boring compared to my friends. Mum always tells me I'm too old.'

Georgia, now 17, who cares for her mother, Australia

Source: Becker (1995b); Price (1996)

In both research and policy for young carers, Britain is more developed than other countries, with a number of national organisations (notably the Carers National Association, Barnardo's, NCH Action for Children and Crossroads) lobbying for and developing services. As we saw in Chapter 3, by mid 1995, there were about 40 young carers projects in Britain (Dearden & Becker, 1995b). By 1997, the number had risen to more than 100 schemes (Aldridge & Becker, 1998).

In all the countries studied, the fear that children might be removed from their family environment was found to be a factor explaining the unwillingness of parents and children alike to talk about their problems to social workers and other service providers who might have been in a position to help them. However, the researchers all found that carers and care-receivers were pleased, even relieved, to be able to discuss their worries with somebody prepared to listen sympathetically.

The long-term consequences of caring on the physical, mental and social well-being of children are not yet fully understood, since most studies of carers have focused on adults (Twigg *et al.*, 1990; Glendinning, 1992). Nonetheless, the findings of the small studies conducted in France, Sweden and Germany, and confirmed by British research, suggest that many young and ex-young carers do experience physical injury as a consequence of lifting their parents during childhood (Aldridge & Becker 1993a; Brittain, 1995; Dietz & Clasen, 1995; Gould, 1995). It is also clear that some young carers require therapeutic interventions during or after their caring experience. Research in France is beginning to show what the long-term effect of caring among siblings may be when a brother or sister has mental health problems (Scelles, 1994; Boucher & Frischmann, 1994).

The young carers studied by these various authors all live under different welfare systems, with a different balance between state provision and family support. Some are the main carer; some share the care with other family members, or with paid welfare professionals. All the young carers, however, experience some restriction to their childhood experience and psychosocial development. While some elements of the caring experience can have a positive impact, these are generally outweighed by the negative effects and consequences which restrict a child's ability to participate fully in many of the roles and activities that are perhaps taken for granted by other children who do not have caring responsibilities.

The evidence presented by Gould, Brittain, and Dietz and Clasen also supports the conclusions of other researchers (Aldridge & Becker, 1993a, 1994; Dearden & Becker, 1995a) that drawing distinctions between levels of caring (primary, secondary, intimate, etc.) may not be helpful in a national or cross-national perspective. It seems more appropriate to define young carers by the impact that caring has upon their childhood, education and psychosocial development (see also Chapter 1). In Britain, while the Carers Act 1995 defines a carer by reference to the amount of care provided, there is now some acknowledgement in the *Practice Guide* to the Act that, in the case of young carers at least, there is a need to consider whether a child's development is impaired as a result of their caring responsibilities, even when they are not providing substantial and regular care (see Chapter 2 for a fuller discussion of this issue).

Young carers in Australia and elsewhere

A number of other developed countries are beginning to acknowledge the issue of young carers and some are starting to construct research strategies to try and 'count' the number of young carers and examine the impacts of caring. So, for example, in 1996/97, welfare agencies in Ireland and Malta initiated a literature review on young carers with the intention of moving on to estimate the numbers of children who take on care-giving roles. In addition, Malta has conducted some small-scale qualitative research within its Social Welfare Development Programme, and, in 1997, convened a seminar on young carers for policy makers, government ministers and welfare practitioners.

Health and nursing researchers in Israel have established a research programme to 'investigate the relationships between the child's involvement in the physical and emotional care of the child's ill mother and between the child's social activities related to friendships, involvement in social frameworks and feelings of loneliness' (Krulik *et al.*, 1997). As with Malta, Israeli researchers have convened a series of seminars on young carers during 1998 which are intended to raise awareness and encourage policy development.

In the United States there is also recognition by a few researchers (again from a nursing discipline) of the role that children play in care-giving. Marie Gates and Nancy Lackey have examined the impact of care-giving on youngsters looking after adults with cancer (Gates & Lackey, in press a, b), while research conducted by Diane Beach focused on the impact of family care-giving on children in situations where a parent has Alzheimer's Type Dementia (ATD). Beach's quali-tative small scale studies (1994, 1997) were of adolescents (with an average age of 18) affected by ATD in the family, rather than specifi-cally about young carers. The adolescent's were all in families where there were other care-givers, although most of the adolescents also helped provide care, usually to a grandparent, parent or aunt/uncle, in that order. Beach suggests that adolescents who were care-givers were 'frustrated with the transient nature of their own peer relationships; they felt compelled to repeatedly remind friends of their caregiving responsibilities and the unavoidable implications for activity time, mood swings and the myriad of other day to day constraints' (Beach, 1994: p. 17). Moreover:

'Feeling unable to fully explain the ATD victim's behaviour, most respondents also felt uncomfortable having friends in their home environments. In terms of school-based support, most respondents reported their teachers and counselors were unaware of their situa-tions at home. While additional attention from school officials may be warranted, it must be handled carefully. These data suggest that a sense of ambivalence regarding potential assistance is common among this population...'

(Beach, 1994: p. 17)

Australia is one of the few other developed countries where there is some information already available on young (and adult) carers. His-torically, the Australian welfare state was based on the premise of achieving a measure of income security and equality through the wages systems, what Castles (1985) refers to as a 'wage earners' welfare state', although Bryson (1992) prefers the term 'white, male wage earners' welfare state'. From 1907, the industrial relations system required businesses to pay a 'living wage' capable of keeping a family in 'frugal comfort'.

Castles and Mitchell (1992) have suggested that the strong labour movement in Australia and the early achievement of a measure of equality through the central control of the employment system set Australia apart from other 'liberal' welfare states, such as those of the USA, the UK and Canada. Liberal welfare states are generally characterised by means-tested benefits, a reduction in the importance of insurance-related benefits, and financial incentives for those who contract out of the state system. These welfare states generally assume responsibility only when the market has failed. Castles and Mitchell argue that this does not apply to Australia, hence their assertion that it is a 'radical liberal' welfare state.

During 13 years of an Australian Labor government, ending in 1996, policies of 'economic rationalism' were pursued, consonant with an international trend towards economic liberalism. While these policies were tempered by some of the more traditional agendas of the political left and Labor's close association with the labour movement, economic efficiency was nonetheless assumed to be attained through enhancing the free play of the markets. This was pursued through deregulation, privatisation, taxation cuts, reductions in public expenditure, and greater targeting of benefits – very similar to the UK (Bryson, 1996). These economic rationalist policies have, Bryson argues, set in train the 'deradicalising' of the Australian welfare system. With a Conservative coalition government taking power in 1996, many of the changes introduced by Labor are expected to 'mature' under the Conservatives, unconstrained by Labor's residual commitment to a social democratic agenda and alongside a range of anti-labour measures (Bryson, 1996). Consequently, it seems likely that Australia's welfare state will move much closer to Esping-Andersen's (1990) notion of a 'liberal' welfare state, a movement similar to that in Britain under both the Con-servatives and New Labour (Becker, 1997). As in Britain, the Aus-tralian system relies heavily on the family as the main providers of care, assisted by a number of cash payments and support services.

The Australian Bureau of Statistics (ABS) calculated that, in 1993, there were 577 500 principal 'adult' carers aged 15 years and over who cared for a person with a 'handicap'. This represented 4.2% of the Australian population aged 15 years and over. Of the total number of carers, 64% were women and 35% were men (Castles, 1993).

In terms of *young* carers (defined here as people under 15 years of age), the ABS calculated that there were 33 800 young carers in Aus-tralia, of which 48% were male. Because the official Australian statistics consider young carers to be those children under 15 years (rather than under 18, as in the European working definition), it would be expected that the ABS figures would reveal a lower number of children involved in care-giving in Australia.

The ABS also estimated that 28 700 (85%) of Australian young carers were in the 10–14 age group and that 17 900 (53%) had the *main* responsibility for at least one task (personal care, health care, help with mobility, home maintenance, meal preparation, financial man-agement, home help, etc.). While just under two thirds of young carers performed only one of these tasks, 22% performed two tasks, 11% performed three tasks and 5% performed four tasks. Additionally, the data show that 23% of young carers in Australia cared for their father, 48% cared for their mother, 21% cared for a brother, 9% for a sister and 13% for a grandparent. Of the total, 13% of young carers in Australia cared for more than one person in the family (ABS, unpublished; see also Carers Association of Australia Inc., 1997: pp. 22–23).

In 1994, the Alzheimer's Association of South Australia received funding from the National Action Plan for Dementia Care to run a Demonstration Project aimed at reducing the stress levels of children who had a parent with dementia and to increase their ability to 'manage' their situation. Some of these children had care-giving roles within the family even if they were not defined as the main or sole carer. The programme was evaluated and led to the publication of a modest report (Alzheimer's Association, 1995) designed to help professionals working with children in these circumstances. This study shows how dementia affects the whole family, including children who may have to take on caring roles: 'For the children, after facing the anxiety generated by the ambiguous nature of the early symptoms, comes the gradual, inevitable loss of their parent. As the dementia progresses the need to provide a significant amount of the nurturing and care in the family often falls on their shoulders...' (Alzheimer's Association, 1995: p. 7).

The Alzheimer's Association study is not a study of young carers *per se*. However, it does show how caring responsibilities among children can change and increase over time. Moreover, it was one of the first studies in Australia which intentionally set out to highlight these issues among welfare professionals who, it was acknowledged, had failed to recognise the role of children in these situations: 'The valuable research into the effects on the carer has been predominantly focused on the adult caregiver, very little has specifically addressed the issues for children and adolescents and early onset dementia' (Alzheimer's Association, 1995: p. 7). Since the publication of this report, the Alzheimer's Association of South Australia has continued to run retreats and camps for children who are in this situation.

A later Australian study focused specifically on 93 'children and young people living in New South Wales, aged 18 years or under or still in secondary school, who provide significant care to an adult with a disability in their household' (Price, 1996: p. 7). In this study 'significant care' was defined as 'the primary provision of assistance to an adult, in areas such as cooking, cleaning, laundry, showering, dressing, toileting, shopping, banking, and caring for other children, beyond what is generally expected from a child of comparable age. The emphasis is on the impact this role may have in restricting the young person's education, leisure and friendships' (Price, 1996: p. 7).

Price discovered that 44% of young carers whose gender was known were male, consistent with the ABS estimate for the national profile of young carers. Three quarters of young carers in Price's study were from lone parent families, 20% from two parent families and 5% lived with a grandparent (for whom they provided care). Almost half the young carers were providing care to an adult with a physical impairment, 19% to someone with a mental health problem and 5% to someone with a sensory disability. Most young carers were providing care for between 10 and 20 hours each week, although some were on call for 24 hours per day. These Australian data are similar to the profile of young carers in Britain described by Dearden and Becker (1995a). In that study 39% of 641 young carers were boys, 60% lived in lone parent families, 60% cared for a parent with a physical impairment, 29% cared for an adult with a mental health problem, and 4% for a person with a sensory disability. One in ten British young carers was caring for more than one person, compared to a figure of one in eight in the Australian national profile (Dearden & Becker, 1995a; ABS, unpublished).

While the statistics may vary between countries, the overall findings and conclusions of the Australian studies are almost identical to those from Britain, France, Sweden and Germany (Aldridge & Becker, 1993a; Becker, 1995b; Dearden & Becker, 1995a). In terms of the *impacts* of caring on children, the Australian research concluded that:

> 'Some young people who live with an adult with a disability may be required to spend many hours assisting the adult with housework or the adult's personal care. The responsibilities undertaken by these young people impact upon many areas of their lives, including their education, friendships, leisure options and the relationships with their family members. These [young] people receive little assistance from community support services. Young people indicated a willingness to accept extra help, but were frustrated by isolation and other barriers.'

> (Price, 1996: p. 4)

Moreover, a study by the Carers Association of Australia outlines some of the long-term consequences of children taking on heavy care responsibilities:

> 'Our consultation with adults who had care responsibilities as children reveals the long term damage that can be caused by heavy care responsibilities and premature "adulthood". Many of the responses from adults who had had care responsibilities as children were filled with bitterness, resentment and a feeling of being "all cared out". Children and young people's lives can be ruined by the heavy burden of family care. Too heavy responsibilities assumed too early in life can damage the lives of young Australians...'

> (Carers Association of Australia Inc., 1997: p. 9)

In terms of the *support needs* of young carers and their families, the Australian research also confirms the British and European findings: 'It is largely in the absence of other support that young people become carers of an adult with a disability' (Price, 1996: p. 26). Many Australian welfare professionals had not identified young carers, and thus failed to engage with their particular needs: 'Their [the professional] focus remained on the adult with the disability, without reflecting how the adult's disability may impact on the functioning of the entire household' (Price, 1996: p. 11). Consequently, 'services must firstly recognise not only the need of the adult but *the needs of the family* as a whole' (p. 26, emphasis in original). As a consequence of this and other local research, the Carers Association of New South Wales has developed an ambitious programme of work for young carers and their families, including an information pack for young carers and a training package for service providers and teachers. The Association is also piloting two other forms of support to young carers, one through local support groups and the other through group counselling over the telephone. Moreover, the Ritz-Carlton Hotel Company has adopted support for young carers in New South Wales as its 'charity of choice' and is involved in funding a number of new initiatives. The Carers Association of Australia has also made a number of recommendations to government which would lead to more recognition and support for children with care responsibilities (Carers Association of Australia Inc., 1997).

Young carers and family obligations

The lack of research in different countries makes it difficult to determine whether the phenomenon is more widespread in one socio-cultural context than another. However, it is possible to draw together a few conclusions based on research in the four European countries studied by Becker (1995b), and in Malta, Australia, the United States and elsewhere, and to attempt to compare the findings to the societal frameworks outlined earlier.

In Britain, young carers have been identified in *official* documents from the mid 1990s, with reference being made to them in Department of Health publications (DoH, 1996b, 1996c; ONS, 1996) and the Carers Act 1995. In the absence of a tradition of explicit family policy, the rights, needs and protection of children – both as children and as carers – have been built into the legal framework, particularly the Children Act 1989 and the Carers Act 1995 (see Chapter 2). Children have the legal right to physical and mental well-being, education, leisure and a secure family environment. When children take on responsibility for a sick or disabled person, many of these rights are undermined, and provisions for children in need or at risk should theoretically be set in motion.

Researchers in Britain (Aldridge & Becker, 1993a, 1994) and in

Australia (Price, 1996) have shown that intervention by public authorities is justified, but they question the form it takes. The approach of public policy makers is ambivalent: state intervention in the private lives of individuals is often stigmatising and can be inter- preted as an identification of personal inadequacy or punishment. Home care services are becoming increasingly well developed but they tend to focus on the sick or disabled person or on adult carers, rather than children. The communication channels between young carers, parents receiving care and professionals (general practitioners, home helps, nurses and social workers) are often far from satisfactory, and researchers continue to recommend better co-ordination of support services which focus on the needs of children who care *and* the whole family.

In Germany, the emphasis in policy on normative behaviour within the conjugal relationship, and the duties which it entails for family members, are not tolerant of non-conformity. Adults are held finan- cially responsible for dependants. The institution of care insurance was the outcome of a long and arduous process of negotiation and debate, but no reference was made to young carers. In a social context where recourse to external help from social services bears a stigma, and where the cost of private services is prohibitive, the presence of a woman in the home and the notion of family responsibility have tended to make families look inwards and to be reluctant to seek help from outside. In the future it seems likely that intervention from external services will be more readily accepted with the institution of care insurance, based as it is, on the concept of individual responsibility (Hantrais & Becker, 1995).

In France and Sweden, where family policies are more explicit and state intervention is more readily accepted and legitimated, current provision would, at first sight, appear to enable children to cope with caring situations without facing the same difficulties as children in Britain or Germany. The research carried out in Sweden by Gould (1995) lends support to this view: he cites examples of generous and sensitive support for children in their own right when their parents are suffering from a 'socially acceptable' illness or disability. In cases of drug and alcohol misuse or AIDS, children in Sweden, Germany, France and Britain, irrespective of the social protection system in operation or family policy objectives and priorities, are generally unable to find the support they need because of the stigma associated with these conditions (Hantrais & Becker, 1995; Newton & Becker, 1996). In Britain, a few specialist young carers projects have been established to support young carers in families where there are mental health problems (Dearden & Becker, 1995b; Aldridge & Becker, 1998.

The responses to young carers appear to differ from one country to another in accordance with their socio-political frameworks. In Britain and Australia, one of the main issues has been concerned with the level of responsibility that children should have in the home and the age at which it is reasonable for them to take on caring duties. In France, emphasis has been on making resources available to ensure that a sick or disabled person can be cared for in his/her own home (including hospital care brought into the home, *hospitalisation à domicile*), so that children should not have to perform heavy caring duties. In Sweden, where the practical needs of children are catered for to a large extent by social and other services, the emotional needs of children still need to be addressed to help them in situations where parental physical impairment or mental ill health is a feature of family life. In Germany, the question is posed in different terms, since caring has long been considered primarily as a moral and ethical duty for family members. The decision to create care insurance within the social insurance system, covering the long-term care needs of sick and elderly people, reinforces the idea of individual responsibility, thereby releasing the state and families from the 'burden' of care provision.

In all the countries studied young carers remain a 'hidden' group. However, it is increasingly clear that the 'phenomenon' of young carers is an international one, regardless of how developed a particular country's welfare system is, or how interventionist their state, or how explicit or implicit their family policy. It is also clear that young caring has not hitherto been identified as a cause for concern. This is perhaps changing as researchers highlight the experiences of young carers in different countries, emphasise the deficiencies in current service arrangements in meeting young carers' needs, and identify the long-term implications of allowing caring among children to continue unrecognised or unchallenged. Awareness-raising strategies in all countries will need to be developed if young carers' issues are to be identified as a cause for concern and action. At the moment, such awareness is far more developed in Britain than elsewhere and it is only Britain which has made substantial progress in identifying and responding to young carers' specific needs. Hantrais and Becker (1995) suggest that it is only after awareness-raising strategies have been employed that the type of welfare mix and the balance between state provision and family support will become more important in determining the kinds of support that young carers will receive, and the source of that support.

Ways forward – the international context

The lack of adequate data on informal caring (Jani-Le Bris, 1993) and children (Ruxton, 1996) in all countries, particularly European Member States, hinders informed discussion of the extent, nature and impact of young caring. Research is required to generate and maintain a more comprehensive database on patterns of informal care-giving and child-related issues, to inform policy and service responses. In 1996, the Parliamentary Assembly of the Council of Europe recommended in its European Strategy for Children that Member States should, as one element of a strategy to make children's rights a priority, make children more visible 'through the systematic collection of information, in particular reliable, detailed (by age and gender), comparable statistics which will make it possible to identify their needs and the issues which require priority political action' (quoted in Ruxton, 1996: p. 14). In Britain there is already some movement towards this goal. Progress has also been made in Australia, with the compilation of some national statistics on young carers and the first published reports on the experiences of young carers and other children affected by their parent's illness (ABS, unpublished; Alzheimer's Association, 1995; Price, 1996; Carers Association of Australia Inc., 1997). Further Australian research and publications are in progress. In France, Sweden and Germany, the work of Brittain (1995), Dietz and Clasen (1995) and Gould (1995) may be credited with having generated interest in the research community and in the specialised associations set up to help care-receivers rather than care-givers, but the issue has not yet reached the mainstream policy agenda. In other countries, notably Malta and Israel, there is now greater awareness of the issues and some attempt to formulate policies to meet the needs of young carers. In the United States nursing researchers have begun to explore the impact of care-giving on adolescents in families where there is Alzheimer's disease or cancer (Beach, 1994, 1997; Gates & Lackey, in press a, b).

Hantrais and Becker (1995) argue that researchers, welfare organisations and professionals in all countries have a strategic role to play in developing awareness, public policy and services for young carers. Whether the development of these services will be at a state or local level has yet to be seen. In Britain, where recognition of young carers is most developed, initiatives have been introduced at the local level which are receptive to local needs, often financed by statutory health or social service authorities but provided by the voluntary (not for profit) sector. Young carers in Britain, it seems, prefer to receive help and support, information and other services from professionals in the voluntary sector because there is less perceived threat or danger of families being split up (DoH, 1996b).

Moreover, as the British and Australian research shows, welfare professionals have an important role to play in supporting young carers *and their families* (Aldridge & Becker, 1993a, 1994; Price, 1996). There is a need to remove the fear that many young carers and their families experience in relation to the statutory caring agencies. Before services are developed at the local level, and before young carers and their families will want to be identified and helped, work must be done to create a less threatening and more enabling climate. All the studies identified a need for better co-operation, co-ordination and networking between sectors, professions and welfare organisations.

The shape of welfare policy relevant to young carers and their families is largely determined by the legislation concerning children, families and carers. It is this legislation that will need to recognise the issue of young caring, and determine the appropriate balance between protecting young carers' childhood and welfare, and/or enabling them to fulfil responsibilities as family carers. In Britain, as we saw in Chapter 2, this has been achieved through a combination of laws: young carers can be assessed under legislation aimed at identifying the needs of carers (the Carers Act 1995) but have their needs met under legislation (the Children Act 1989) which defines them as children in need. Some countries may wish to introduce strategies to try and prevent young caring. Where children are involved in caring practices that deprive them of some aspects of their childhood, services need to be developed to help young carers and their parents. At the same time, a preventative strategy may also be developed to reduce the likelihood that some children will be 'elected' or drawn into the caring role, and to reduce the vulnerability of some children in particular (for example, a single child in a family with a long-term sick or disabled lone parent). However, it is likely that there will always be children who fall through any preventative safety net, and these children will also need support and protection (Aldridge & Becker, 1997; see also Chapter 3).

Achieving the right balance between prevention and intervention remains problematic and yet it is central to the relationship between parents and children who care, and between individuals, families and the state. It is the responsibility of each state to determine this balance. Hantrais and Becker (1995) argue, however, that there is a matter of common principle involved here that cuts across national boundaries, namely the rights of *all* children to a safe and secure childhood. As discussed in Chapter 2, the 1989 UN Convention on the Rights of the Child recognises that children are holders of a specific set of identifiable rights. The Convention consists of 54 Articles, many of which are directly relevant to children with care-giving roles. In 1990, the World Summit on Children endorsed the emphasis on the 'rights' of children, stating that: 'The well-being of children requires political action at the highest level. We are determined to take that action. We ourselves make a solemn commitment to give priority to the rights of children' (quoted in Ruxton, 1996: p. 1).

Hantrais and Becker (1995) argue that the UN Convention provides an opportunity to develop a cross-national framework for securing the rights of young carers. It can also be used as a yardstick against which international policy and service developments can be measured. The Council of Europe European Strategy for Children, adopted in 1996, advocates a set of measures to make children's rights a political priority in Member States of the Council of Europe (Ruxton, 1996: p. 26). Member States are encouraged to take a number of steps, including:

- guaranteeing, through explicit recognition in their constitutional texts or domestic law, the civil and political rights of children as enshrined in the UN Declaration on the Rights of the Child;
- guaranteeing all children the right to a high level of education;
- informing children of their rights;
- informing children about the means and remedies available to them in the event of the violation of their fundamental rights;
- providing specific training in children's rights for all professionals who come into contact with children; and
- enabling the views of children to be heard in all decision-making which affects them.

These measures raise important issues for both policy and practice relating to young carers and their families, some of which have already been examined in Chapter 3.

Conclusion

From the studies conducted in Britain, France, Sweden, Germany, Australia and the United States, it is clear that, irrespective of the nature of each country's welfare system, young carers have been largely ignored by researchers, policy makers and practitioners. It is only since the early 1990s that this situation has begun to change in some countries. Britain and Australia are further ahead in recognising the issue of young carers and in conducting research and responding to needs. Others, such as Malta, Sweden, Germany, France, Israel and the United States, have begun to be aware of the issue but this is still in its infancy. Ireland, Malta and Israel are also just beginning to conduct preliminary research on the extent and nature of young caring in their respective countries, following their reviews of the largely British literature on young carers. However, in most developed nations, the issue of children as care-givers has not yet emerged at all onto the research, policy or practice agenda.

Young carers are an international phenomenon. All of those countries which have conducted any research on the issue have identified the issue, even though young caring had not previously been recognised as a cause for concern. That individual countries should 'find' young carers once they started looking should come as no surprise. The family is the cornerstone of care in the community in most developed and non-developed countries and, in some circumstances, children will have to take on care responsibilities. The recognition of this, and whether or not young carers' needs are identified and met, seems to rely heavily on the commitment, projects and strategies of researchers and other individuals and organisations whose work raises awareness of the issue and helps place it on the policy agenda. Only after awareness has been raised will the type of each country's welfare system, and the balance between state provision and family support, become important in determining the nature and source of support for young carers and their families.

Chapter 5

Conclusions: Working Together for Young Carers and their Families

Introduction

In the final chapter we draw together some of the main themes of the book and offer a number of conclusions. It is our contention that to move forward for the benefit of young carers *and* their families, and before professionals can work effectively together for children and parents in these families, we need to consider young caring in the context of 'childhood' and 'caring', and the tensions and contradictions therein. We also consider how professionals might best provide family support to young carers and their ill or disabled parents, support which enables all family members to achieve autonomy, independence and security.

The sociology of childhood

The dominant sociological discourse defines childhood as a social rather than a biological construct (Aries, 1962; James & Prout, 1997). Indeed, during the last decade or so there has been a growing literature which can be broadly defined as a 'sociology of childhood'. The features of this literature are:

> 'that childhood should be studied in its own right; that children should be the units of observation; that children should themselves talk about their own experiences; that childhood should be seen as a part of social structure; that children should be studied in the present not only in relation to their future as adults; that childhood be seen in an intergenerational context.'

> (Qvortrup, 1996: p. xi)

Traditionally, children have been seen in family sociology but not meant to be heard (James & Prout, 1996: p. 41). However, the emerging sociology of childhood has challenged traditional views about family and childhood – it has been about 'wrestling the study of children out of the familial context of socialisation within which, for so many years, it was traditionally located' (James & Prout, 1996: p. 41). Children are being conceptually liberated from a passive dependency on adults, and elevated to the status of competent social actors. In the sociology of childhood children are attributed with agency and purpose (Brannen & O'Brien, 1996: p. 1; James & Prout, 1996: p. 42).

James and Prout have argued that age is one of the key features in understanding how we construct the notion of childhood: '... concepts of age are the main scaffolding around which western conceptions of childhood are built and it is through reference to concepts of age that the daily life experiences of children are produced and controlled' (1990: p. 222). Thus, childhood is presented and internalised not only as a 'state of being' but also as a 'state of becoming', a preparation for maturity, adulthood, middle age and, ultimately, old age itself (Newman, 1996: p. 6).

Newman has further argued that the parameters of childhood – as defined by the age of majority – are shifted periodically according to fashion, beliefs and knowledge.

> 'Childhood, as defined by these age-related criteria, has been both lengthened (education, sex, working) and shortened (voting, marrying). At present, children are held responsible in law for their actions at 10, can own an air rifle at 14, may leave school, buy cigarettes, work full-time and have sex with a heterosexual partner at 16, join the armed forces at 17, and purchase alcohol and vote at 18.'
>
> (Newman, 1996: p. 7)

In almost every country, age limits formally regulate children's activities. Across the world there are different ages at which children can be involved in work and other tasks or responsibilities (Bellamy, 1997: p. 25). However, the elimination of these age distinctions has been seen by some children's rights advocates as a prerequisite for children's liberation (Franklin, 1986). For other children's rights advocates, childhood and adulthood are seen as separate but linked domains requiring some demarcation, most often by age or some judgement about a child's level of maturity. Stressing children's developmental progression, this 'moderate' children's rights perspective sees children as both vulnerable *and* needing autonomy. Children are seen as being fully equal to adults as persons, 'and yet it would be maltreatment to burden them with fully equal responsibilities' (Fox Harding, 1997: p. 122). Most of the children's charities in the UK take this 'moderate' perspective, constructing childhood as both a 'state of being' and a 'state of becoming'. Children are seen as needing both protection and rights to participation; these needs are also an inherent feature of much of the young carers literature. The UN Convention sites the child's locus of independence and autonomy in his or her level of maturity and decision-making capacity, rather than in age, although there is no widely accepted model available for assessing the capacity of children to make mature and autonomous decisions. Consequently, most countries adopt age as a means of distinguishing between childhood and adulthood, irrespective of the maturity of the individual child or their capacity for independent decision-making.

Childhood and caring: tensions and contradictions

We need to recognise that caring *for* and caring *about* other people is something that most if not all children are encouraged to do during childhood. It is part of their socialisation and is a prerequisite for healthy psychosocial development, and it is considered a beneficial part of growing up (beneficial to children and to wider and adult society). We (as parents, teachers, adults) encourage children throughout childhood to adopt a caring disposition and to value caring and being 'helpful'. Most, if not all children *will* care about and for others, within and outside their families, as part of their routine childhood development, and this caring needs to be encouraged and nurtured if children are to value caring during childhood and in adult life. Many children *will* help parents (disabled or non-disabled) in the home, with household tasks, child care, or fetching and watching over siblings.

But what of children who take on tasks or responsibilities that have an *impact* on their own development and opportunities to engage fully in the breadth of experience that constitutes childhood? We have defined this particular group of children as 'young carers' and it is they who have been the focus of this book. Our work and the work of others – which is part of the growing literature on the sociology of childhood – has studied children as carers in their own right; has given them a voice; has regarded them as social actors. However, while young carers are competent in their caring roles, they are still dependent in terms of their status as children. Although to some extent their roles confer purpose, unsupported and isolated these children have little power.

The new welfare category of 'young carer' enables us to differentiate (conceptually and practically through the development of policy and the provision of services) between children whose experience of caring is a beneficial and routine part of childhood development, and where caring is of a quite different nature and level, and where the *impact* on a child's development and transition to adulthood is negative or damaging. Young carers are essentially children whose participation in caring is of a more exaggerated nature, for whatever reason, than routine caring or 'being helpful' among other children. The restrictions this imposes on their childhoods are exacerbated by the failure of welfare professionals and organisations to support children and parents.

Another consequence for young carers is the negative impact on their development and transition from childhood to adulthood. The aspects of a child's development that may be endangered by caring and a lack of appropriate professional support include their physical development (overall health, co-ordination, etc.), cognitive development (including the acquisition of knowledge necessary to normal life), emotional development (including adequate self esteem), and social development (including a sense of peer group identity) (Bellamy, 1997: pp. 24–5). The pattern and routes of transition from childhood to adulthood can also be compromised: 'Transition to adulthood is the process by which young people move away from dependence for primary, emotional and financial support from their childhood family or carers...' (Garrett, 1996: p. 9). The process of transition happens in different ways and at different rates for individual young people, but Garrett (1996) identifies its major constituents as:

- Transition from school to training, employment or unemployment
- Moving out of the parents'/carers' home
- Transition to adult sexuality, coupledom, marriage and possibly parenthood
- Financial independence from parents.

Clearly, young caring can distort these transition patterns: 'illness, disability or family problems can all interrupt the process of gaining the knowledge and skills which allow young people to get jobs, to make relationships and find somewhere to live' (Garrett, 1996: p. 9).

Thus, young carers' experiences of caring challenge common understanding of what childhood is about. Because young carers are often involved in adult-like tasks which require maturity, responsibility and often a high degree of expertise, there is a question as to whether it is appropriate for children to be involved in such tasks at all, or whether there are appropriate ages at which children might be reasonably expected to take on these responsibilities. So, for example, at what age should children be allowed to toilet a parent or to carry them up and down stairs? Could we define an age for these and other tasks or responsibilities? Even if it was possible to determine an 'appropriate' age, would it be desirable to do so?

Children themselves have some answers to these questions. In the first national survey of young people's social attitudes children identified a hierarchy of age-related milestones, progressing from making one's own bed and helping with the washing up at around ten years, to getting a part-time job at 14, to baby-sitting for a child of five at 16, to marriage and voting at 18 years (Roberts & Sachdev, 1996). While no questions were asked specifically about the age at which young people should take on caring roles and responsibilities, the data indicate that young people themselves do accept the notion of age-related rights, although as we would expect there are variations in attitudes between the different age bands and genders.

'... young people appear to acquiesce in the widely accepted adult premise that certain activities should be forbidden to children until a particular age has been attained, although some disparity may exist as to what this age should actually be... Children, it appears, still recognise their vulnerability and feel the need to be protected from certain activities (or not be expected to undertake them) until a particular age has been reached.'

(Newman, 1996: pp. 9–10)

Given that most young people cited 16 as the age at which children should be allowed to baby-sit for a child of five, then what are the implications of this for children's involvement in other, more intimate caring roles? The children surveyed had some ideas about what con-stitutes 'adult' responsibility and what is more appropriate for children to undertake. We could therefore conclude that the nature of many young carers' responsibilities could be called into question by children themselves.

However, the logistics of defining age-related milestones for specific caring tasks or responsibilities are profoundly problematic. People will always have different views about 'appropriate age' and age-appropriate behaviour. Moreover, it would be almost impossible (and largely undesirable) to 'police' any such age limits for caring tasks within the family. Family life, particularly in the UK, is seen as a private domain except when the interests and welfare of children are threat-ened. Consequently, the tendency in social policy has been to intervene as little as possible in family arrangements (Hantrais, 1994; Millar & Warman, 1996).

At the very least, in our view, children should not have to perform dangerous physical tasks or take on emotionally distressing responsi-bilities during childhood (i.e. before the age of 18). Children and par-ents should have choices regarding the caring arrangements within their family. In reality, many children do have to care and will continue to do so, just as their parents are also often forced to receive care from their children. Professionals have a key role to play here in determining the quality of life of these children and parents.

Young caring in an intergenerational context

It is important to understand young caring as one aspect of inter-generational caring, reciprocity and interdependence. Jan Walmsley (1993) argues that care and dependence are false dichotomies. Walmsley makes the case for viewing care as a continuum, 'more complex than a straight division between carer and dependent allows' (1993: p. 131), and notes that: 'We are all dependent to a greater or lesser degree on others. And so-called dependants can themselves be carers ... To some extent, who is the carer is in the eye of the beholder' (Walmsley, 1993: pp. 131–35). A number of other researchers have challenged the received wisdom that there is a clear distinction between carer and 'dependant' (Bogdan & Taylor, 1989; Oliver, 1989; Morris, 1991), arguing, as we do in Chapter 3, that their interests need to be addressed together.

Ill or disabled parents may receive care but they can also provide care to their children and to others. Both sides gain from the continuation of the family structure and relationships, enhanced by the exchange of caring, rather than its fracture when children are taken away from parents or parents are hospitalised. The reciprocal and interdependent nature of the caring relationship enables the family to survive as a unit. It allows young carers and their families to go on living, loving and working together as a *family*. Morris contends that we need to re-focus research and policy not so much on 'carers' as on 'caring', and that doing this will show the interdependence of all those involved in a caring relationship (Morris, 1991). However, as far as young carers are concerned, we would argue that it is imperative that the focus on *children* as carers is maintained, as opposed to shifting attention to 'caring' *per se*. The *young carers* distinction is important if we are to safeguard the integrity of children and address their needs as carers.

Welfare professionals and the state

Throughout this book we have argued that it is the availability and type of care provided by welfare professionals which will be a key factor in determining the quality of life of young carers and care receivers, their levels of independence and autonomy, and ultimately whether some children become carers or not.

Our approach also implies a particular view about the role of government and the objectives of social policy – an explicitly interventionist and collectivist paradigm, rather than one which leaves families alone to look after each other, as occurs in some southern European states and elsewhere (see Chapter 4). To adopt Millar and Warman's (1996) classification (see Chapter 4), we would argue that the British government's strategy towards carers and their families must move from a position of 'no clear state responsibility' to one of 'clear state responsibility'. Here, the state's obligations to citizens with care needs and to carers (young or adult) need to be made clear *and* explicit, and the aims of social policy and services should be to value autonomy and independence within a context of family diversity and difference. At the same time we must not deny the critical contribution made by the voluntary and private sectors. While we argue for a strong collectivist and explicit role for the state, we also recognise the importance and value of a range of services from a mixed economy of welfare. Indeed, many young carers and their families may prefer to receive services from the voluntary sector (or from the private sector if they could afford them). Most of the young carers projects in the UK are voluntary agencies even though they receive some funding from the state (from local authorities). Some projects receive funding from private corporate sponsors and there is room for more developments of this type. Moreover, as argued in Chapter 3, there is a need for more neighbourhood family centres, again often voluntary sector organisations, to engage with the needs of young carers and their families.

Child protection and family support

As referred to above, it is important for family structure to be maintained as far as possible. However, at the same time professionals need to be aware that in some extreme circumstances, particularly where young carers are in essentially exploitative caring relationships which are resistant to change, child protection procedures may need to be implemented. In such circumstances young carers will have moved along a continuum, from being defined as 'children in need' to being seen as 'children at risk'. In these (rare) situations family support will be the context within which child protection issues arise (Hearn, 1997: p. 231).

Invoking child protection procedures for young carers who are considered to be children at risk should only occur after extensive attempts to support the family have failed. If professionals are truly empowering rather than obstructive, child protection procedures will rarely, if ever , have to be used for young carers and their families. Professionals need to make far greater use of the existing legislation, especially Section 17 of the Children Act (Chapter 2), which gives social services departments the power to provide support to families where children are defined as in need: 'the filter that has been selected, and through which the flow of demand for family support services must pass, is *children in need*' (Tunstill, 1997: p. 48, emphasis in original).

However, since its inception, family support has been given far less priority than child protection. Children in need have received less attention and professional resources than children at risk. Tunstill believes that the root causes of the failure of Section 17 to re-balance the relationship between child protection and family support are the adverse political and economic circumstances in which it has been introduced (Tunstill, 1997: p. 56). As far as young carers and their families are concerned, family support (and supportive family approaches such as family group conferences and family centres, which were discussed in Chapter 3), are critical to the healthy future of families and for the autonomy of all family members.

There remain, however, substantial strategic, resource and practical difficulties that stand in the way of the full implementation of Section

17, despite the call for a re-balancing of child protection work. The report *Child Protection: Messages from Research* (Dartington Social Research Unit, 1995) suggests that greater priority should be given to family support while keeping policing and investigations to a minimum. But, if social services have failed to fully implement family support, even in the context of child neglect and abuse, it seems unlikely that they will make extensive use of it for young carers and their families. Given this uncertainty about the importance of family support on the social services agenda, and the tensions inherent in maintaining an *integrated* child care system which values both family support and child protection, there is some question as to whether these two functions should be divided between different agencies: 'If we are serious about developing child welfare, simple integration may not be the answer. It may be that we have a much better chance of success if we aim to clearly *separate* and *demarcate* responsibilities, resources and lines of accountability' (Parton, 1997: p. 20, emphasis in original). Parton suggests that the policing role of child protection could perhaps be given to another agency (the NSPCC for example) while social services retain the family support function. Conversely, social services could retain the child protection function while a voluntary agency takes on family support.

Frost (1997: p. 196) confirms that the increased emphasis on family support will involve some difficult strategic choices for social services and voluntary organisations about functions and lines of responsibility. The Children Act makes it clear that local authorities can purchase services for family support from voluntary organisations. Frost outlines a model that social services could adopt with regard to voluntary organisations and to the emphasis that social services might want to place on family support. It provides a basis for developing policies on family support for young carers and their families. The options are relatively simple: social services can take a high family support role or contract this function out to voluntary organisations – a mixed economy of welfare as in the community care sphere. Family support might, for example, include greater use of voluntary sector family centres or young carers projects, counselling services, independent co-ordination of family group conferences, and family advocacy schemes (Chapter 3). Arguably, it should also include a greater and more creative use of Section 17 cash payments to young carers' families, to complement other social security benefits and direct payments (Becker, 1997).

One way for social services departments to decide on support strategies for young carers would be for them to seek the views of local young carers and their families to find out which form of family support they would prefer – social services or voluntary agency assistance. Given the evidence that young carers and their families prefer young carers projects to be voluntary rather than statutory, it seems likely that the voluntary sector would be both preferable and better placed to provide non-stigmatising family support to young carers and their families. Once a social services department has consulted and decided on a strategy this should be built into the authority's Children's Services Plans (CSPs): 'There is no doubt that [CSPs] provide the possibility for auditing and developing services and clarifying and negotiating issues at the local level – the key terrain where these debates will be addressed' (Parton, 1997: p. 19). Moreover, as Frost contends: 'The process of devising the plan presents an excellent opportunity for engaging all relevant parties with family support issues and for ensuring that family support plays a central role in the plan' (Frost, 1997: p. 202).

The way forward is to acknowledge, value and respect the reciprocal and interdependent nature of caring between young carers and their families, and to support and nurture these relationships through a range of policies, services and procedures. This will only be possible if both policy and practice become more evidence-based than they are at present (Fuller & Petch, 1995; MacDonald & Roberts 1995). Further research on young carers and their families has a crucial role to play in determining the future direction of policy and practice. There is an urgent need for research strategies which combine a range of disciplines, and which use different research methods, including experimental designs, ethnographic studies and longitudinal surveys. We need to know far more about why some children become young carers in the first place, not only about the processes of negotiation or non-negotiation that take place within the family, but also about how interventions by welfare professionals might reduce the likelihood of some children becoming young carers. Longitudinal studies are useful to discover how young carers' lives and experiences, and their relationships with parents *and* welfare professionals, change through childhood and into adulthood. Further insight is needed into child–parent relationships and interactions in families where a parent has an illness or disability, and how and why some children in these families may *never* take on caring roles while others do. What are the processes which prevent some children ever becoming young carers, and what are the implications for preventative services and policies?

References

Adamson, L., Als, H., Tronick, E. & Brazelton, T.B. (1977) The development of social reciprocity between a sighted infant and her blind parents. *Journal of the American Academy of Child Psychiatry*, 16, 2, 194–207.

Aldgate, J., Tunstill, J., McBeath, G. & Ozolins, R. (1994) *Implementing Section 17 of the Children Act – The first 18 months. A Study for the Department of Health*. University of Leicester, Leicester.

Aldridge, J. & Becker, S. (1993a) *Children who Care: Inside the World of Young Carers*. Young Carers Research Group, Loughborough University, Loughborough.

Aldridge, J. & Becker, S. (1993b) Punishing children for caring. *Children and Society*, 7, 4, 277–88.

Aldridge, J. & Becker, S. (1994) *My Child, My Carer: The Parents' Perspective*. Young Carers Research Group, Loughborough University, Loughborough.

Aldridge, J. & Becker, S. (1995) The rights and wrongs of children who care. In *Children's Rights: A Handbook of Comparative Policy and Practice* (Ed by B. Franklin), pp. 119–30. Routledge, London.

Aldridge, J. & Becker, S. (1996) Disability rights and the denial of young carers: the dangers of zero-sum arguments. *Critical Social Policy*, 16, 55–76.

Aldridge, J. and Becker, S. (1997) *Prevention and Intervention: Young Carers and their Families. A Report for the Calouste Gulbenkian Foundation*. Young Carers Research Group, Loughborough University, Loughborough.

Aldridge, J. and Becker, S. (1998) *The Handbook of Young Carers Projects*. Carers National Association, London.

Alzheimer's Association of South Australia (1995) *My Parent Has Dementia: A Child and Adolescent Perspective*. Alzheimer's Association, South Australia.

Anthony, E.J. (1970) The impact of mental and physical illness on family life. *American Journal of Psychiatry*, 127, 2, 138–46.

Aries, P. (1962) *Centuries of Childhood*. Jonathan Cape, London.

Arnaud, S.H. (1959) Some psychological characteristics of children of multiple sclerotics. *Psychosomatic Medicine*, 21, 1, 8–22.

Association of Metropolitan Authorities (1991) *Children First: Report of the AMA Working Party on Services for Young Children*. AMA, London.

Audit Commission (1992) *Community Care: Managing the Cascade of Change*. HMSO, London.

Australian Bureau of Statistics (ABS) (unpublished) *Carers under 15*. ABS, Australia.

Baldwin, S. & Twigg, J. (1991) Women and community care: reflections on a debate. In *Women's Issues in Social Policy* (Ed by M. Maclean & D. Groves), pp. 117–35. Routledge, London.

Bank-Mikklesen, N. (1980) Denmark. In *Normalisation, Social Integration and Community Services* (Ed by R. J. Flynn & K. E. Nitsch). University Park Press, New York.

Barnes, C. (1992) Discrimination, disability benefits and the 1980s. *Benefits*, 3, 3–7.

Barnes, M. (1997) *Care, Communities and Citizens*. Longman, London.

Beach, D.L. (1994) Family care of Alzheimer victims: an analysis of the adolescent experience. *The American Journal of Alzheimer's Care and Related Disorders & Research*, January/February, 12–19.

Beach, D.L. (1997) Family caregiving: the positive impact on adolescent relationships. *The Gerontologist*, 37, 2, 233–8.

Bean, P. (1980) *Mental Illness: Changes and Trends*. John Wiley and Sons, Chichester.

Becker, S. (1995a) Introduction. In *Young Carers in Europe: An Exploratory Cross-National Study in Britain, France, Sweden and Germany* (Ed by S. Becker), pp. vii–x. Young Carers Research Group in association with the European Research Centre, Loughborough University, Loughborough.

Becker, S. (Ed.) (1995b) *Young Carers in Europe: An Exploratory Cross-National Study in Britain, France, Sweden and Germany*. Young Carers Research Group in association with the European Research Centre, Loughborough University, Loughborough.

Becker, S. (1997) *Responding to Poverty: The Politics of Cash and Care*. Longman, London.

Bellamy, C. (1997) *The State of the World's Children 1997*. Oxford University Press for UNICEF, Oxford.

Berry-Lound, D. & Marsh, K. (1996) *Working and Caring for Older People in Europe: A Three Country Comparison*. Help the Aged, London.

Bilsborrow, S. (1992) *'You grow up fast as well...' Young Carers on Merseyside*. Carers National Association, Personal Services Society and Barnardo's, Liverpool.

Blackford, K.A. (1988) The children of chronically ill parents. *Journal of Psychosocial Nursing*, 26, 3, 33–6.

Bleuler, M. (1978) *The Schizophrenic Disorders: Long Term Patient and Family Studies*. University Press, New Haven.

Bogdan, R. & Taylor, S. (1989) Relationships with severely disabled people: the social construction of humanness. *Social Problems*, 36, 135–48.

Booth, T. & Booth, W. (1997) *Exceptional Childhoods, Unexceptional Children*. Family Policy Studies Centre, London.

Boucher, N. & Frischmann, M. (1994) 'Paroles d'enfants' – La fraitre de l'enfant atteint d'une maladie neuro-musculaire. *Myoline*, 12, 3.

Brannen, J. & O'Brien, M. (1996) Introduction. In *Children and Families: Research and Policy* (Ed by J. Brannen & M. O'Brien), pp. 1–12. Falmer Press, London.

Brisdenen, S. (1986) Independent living and the medical model of disability. *Disability, Handicap and Society*, 1, 2, 173–8.

Brittain, D. (1995) Young carers in France. In *Young Carers in Europe: An Exploratory Cross-National Study in Britain, France, Sweden and Germany* (Ed by S. Becker), pp. 27–47. Young Carers Research Group in association with the European Research Centre, Loughborough University, Loughborough.

Brown, H. & Smith, H. (Eds) (1992) *Normalisation: A Reader for the Nineties*. Routledge, London.

Bryson, L. (1992) *Welfare and the State: Who Benefits?* Macmillan, London.

Bryson, L. (1996) A letter from Australia: transforming Australia's welfare state. *SPA News*, May/June, 11–12.

Buck, F.M. & Hohmann, G.W. (1983) Parental disability and children's adjustment. In *Annual Review of Rehabilitation* (Ed by E.L. Pan, T.E. Backer & C.L. Vash), pp. 203–41. Springer Publishing Co., New York.

Cannan, C. & Warren, C. (1997) Introduction. In *Social Action with Children and Families: A Community Development Approach to Child and Family Welfare* (Ed by C. Cannan & C. Warren), pp. 1–19. Routledge, London.

Carers Association of Australia Inc. (1997) *Questions of Responsibility: Children and Caring in Australia.* Commonwealth of Australia, Canberra.

Carers National Association (1992) *Speak Up, Speak Out.* CNA, London.

Carers National Association (1997) *Still Battling? The Carers Act One Year On.* CNA, London.

Carers (Recognition and Services) Act 1995. HMSO, London.

Castles, F. (1985) *The Working Class and Welfare: Reflections on the Political Development of the Welfare State in Australia and New Zealand, 1890–1980.* Allen and Unwin, Wellington.

Castles, F. & Mitchell, D. (1992) Three worlds of welfare capitalism. *Governance*, 5, 1.

Castles, I. (1993) *Disability, Ageing and Carers, Australia 1993: Summary of Findings.* Australian Bureau of Statistics, Australia.

Castro de la Mata, R., Gingras, G. & Wittkower, E.D. (1960) Impact of sudden, severe disablement of the father upon the family. *Canadian Medical Association Journal*, 82, 1015–20.

Challenge (1992) *A Challenge to Community Care.* Challenge, London.

Children Act 1989. HMSO, London.

Children (Scotland) Act 1995. HMSO, London.

Children's Legal Centre (undated) *The Children Act 1989.* Children's Legal Centre, London.

Children's Rights Development Unit (1994) *UK Agenda for Children.* CRDU, London.

Christ, G.H., Siegal, K., Freund, B., Langosch, D., Hendersen, S., Sperber, D. & Weinstein, L. (1993) Impact of parental terminal cancer on latency-age children. *American Journal of Orthopsychiatry*, 63, 3, 417–25.

Chronically Sick and Disabled Persons Act 1970. HMSO, London.

Clarke, K. (1988) *Statement to Parliament on the Future Arrangements for Community Care.* Department of Health press release, 12 July.

Cogswell, B.E. (1976) Conceptual model of a family as a group: family response to disability. In *The Sociology of Physical Disability and Rehabilitation* (Ed by G.L. Albrecht). University of Pittsburg Press, Pittsburg.

Community Care (Direct Payments) Act 1996. HMSO, London.

Cytryn, L., McKnew, D.H., Bartko, J.J., Lamour, M. & Hamovitt, J. (1982) Offspring of patients with affective disorders: II. *Journal of the American Academy of Child Psychiatry*, 21, 4, 389–91.

Dalley, G. (1988) *Ideologies of Caring: Rethinking Community and Collectivism.* Macmillan, Basingstoke.

Dartington Social Research Unit (1995) *Child Protection: Messages from Research.* HMSO, London.

Davis Smith, J. (Ed.) (1993) *Volunteering in Europe.* The Volunteer Centre, Berkhamstead.

Dearden, C., Aldridge, J., Newton, B. & Becker, S. (1994) *Getting it Right for Young Carers: A Training Pack for Professionals*. Young Carers Research Group, Loughborough University, Loughborough.

Dearden, C. & Becker, S. (1995a) *Young Carers: The Facts*. Reed Business Publishing, Sutton.

Dearden, C. & Becker, S. (1995b) *The National Directory of Young Carers Projects and Initiatives*. Young Carers Research Group, Loughborough University and Carers National Association, Loughborough.

Dearden, C. and Becker, S. (1996) *Young Carers at the Crossroads: An Evaluation of the Nottingham Young Carers Project*. Young Carers Research Group, Loughborough University in association with Crossroads, Loughborough.

Dearden, C. & Becker, S. (1997) *Children in Care, Children who Care: Parental Illness and Disability and the Child Care System. A Report to the Calouste Gulbenkian Foundation*. Young Carers Research Group, Loughborough University, Loughborough.

Dearden, C. & Becker, S. (1998) *A National Survey of Young Carers and the Carers Act*. Carers National Association, London.

Degener, T. (1995) Disabled persons and human rights: the legal framework. In *Human Rights and Disabled Persons: Essays and Relevant Human Rights Instruments* (Ed by T. Degener & Y. Koster-Dreese). Martinus Mijhoff, Holland.

Department of Health (1989a) *Caring for People: Community Care in the Next Decade and Beyond*. HMSO, London.

Department of Health (1989b) *An Introduction to the Children Act 1989*. HMSO, London.

Department of Health (1993) *Caring for People: Information Pack for the Voluntary and Private Sectors*. Department of Health, London.

Department of Health (1996a) *Carers (Recognition and Services) Act 1995: Policy Guidance and Practice Guide*. Department of Health, London.

Department of Health (1996b) *Young Carers: Making a Start*. Department of Health, London.

Department of Health (1996c) *Young Carers: Something to Think About. Report of Four SSI Workshops, May–July 1995*. Department of Health, London.

Department of Health (1996d) *Children Looked After by Local Authorities Year Ending 31 March 1995, England*. HMSO, London.

Department of Health (1997) *Direct Payments Act: Presentation Materials*. Department of Health, London.

Department of Health press release (1992) *Virginia Bottomley Announces Government Support for Community Care*. Department of Health, 2 October.

Department of Health press release (1996) *Refocusing Children's Services*, Department of Health, 26 September.

Dietz, B. & Clasen, J. (1995) Young carers in Germany. In *Young Carers in Europe: An Exploratory Cross-National Study in Britain, France, Sweden and Germany* (Ed by S. Becker), pp. 65–76. Young Carers Research Group in association with the European Research Centre, Loughborough University, Loughborough.

Disabled Persons (Services, Consultation and Representation) Act 1986. HMSO, London.

Elliott, A. (1992) *Hidden Children: A Study of Ex-Young Carers of Parents with Mental Health Problems in Leeds*. Leeds City Council, Mental Health Development Section, Leeds.

Erlenmeyer-Kimling, L., Cornblatt, B., Friedman, D., Marcuse, Y., Rainer, J.D. & Rutschmann, J. (1980) A prospective study of children of schizophrenic parents. *International Journal of Rehabilitation Research*, 3, 1, 90–1.

Esping-Andersen, G.T. (1990) *The Three Worlds of Welfare Capitalism*. Polity Press, Cambridge.

Eurostat (1997) Unpublished tabulations provided by Eurostat from the 1994 European Community Household Panel, initial results.

Fallon, K. (1990) An involuntary workforce. *Community Care*, January 4, 12–13.

Family Rights Group (1991) *The Children Act 1989: Working in Partnership with Families*. HMSO, London.

Feldman, M.A., Case, L., Towns, F. & Betel, J. (1985) Parental education project I: development and nurturance of children of mentally retarded parents. *American Journal of Mental Deficiency*, 90, 3, 253–8.

Feldman, R.A., Stiffman, A.R. & Jung, K.G. (1987) *Children at Risk in the Web of Parental Mental Illness*. Rutgers University Press, New Brunswick and London.

Finch, J. & Groves, D. (1980) Community care and the family: a case for equal opportunities? *Journal of Social Policy*, 9, 4, 487–511.

Fox, N.J. (1995) Professional models of school absence associated with home responsibilities. *British Journal of Sociology of Education*, 16, 2, 221–42.

Fox Harding, L. (1997) *Perspectives in Child Care Policy*. Longman, London.

Frank, J. (1995) *Couldn't Care More: A Study of Young Carers and their Needs*. The Children's Society, London.

Frankenburg, F.R., Sloman, L. & Perry, A. (1985) Issues in the therapy of hearing children with deaf parents. *Canadian Journal of Psychiatry*, 30, 2, 98–102.

Franklin, B. (Ed.) (1986) *The Rights of Children*. Blackwell, London.

Frost, N. (1997) Delivering family support: issues and themes in service development. In *Child Protection and Family Support: Tensions, Contradictions and Possibilities* (Ed by N. Parton), pp. 193–212. Routledge, London.

Fuller, R. (1989) Problems and possibilities in studying preventive work. *Adoption and Fostering*, 13, 1, 9–13.

Fuller, R. & Petch, A. (1995) *Practitioner Research: The Reflexive Social Worker*. Open University Press, Buckingham.

Garrett, L. (1996) Introduction. In *Transition to Adulthood* (Barnardo's Policy Development Unit), pp. 9–11. Barnardo's, Ilford.

Gates, M.F. & Lackey, N.R. (in press, a) Caregiving of adults with cancer by youngsters. *IMAGE: Journal of Nursing Scholarship*.

Gates, M.F. & Lackey, N.R. (in press, b) Combining the analysis of three data sets in studying young caregivers. *Journal of Advanced Nursing*.

George, V. & Taylor-Gooby, P. (1996) *European Welfare Policy: Squaring the Welfare Circle*. Macmillan, London.

Germino, B.B. & Funk, S.G. (1993) Impact of a parent's cancer on adult children: role and relationship issues. *Seminars in Oncology Nursing*, 9, 2, 101–6.

Glendinning, C. (1991) Losing ground: social policy and disabled people in Great Britain 1980–1990. *Disability, Handicap and Society*, 6, 1, 3–17.

Glendinning, C. (1992) *The Costs of Informal Care: Looking Inside the Household*. Social Policy Research Unit/HMSO, London.

Glendinning, C. & McLaughlin, E. (1993) *Paying for Care: Lessons from Europe*. Social Security Advisory Committee Research Paper 5, HMSO, London.

Goffman, E. (1961) *Asylums*. Doubleday, New York.

Goffman, I. (1969) *Stigma: Notes of the Management of Spoiled Identity*. Penguin, London.

Gottesman, I. & Shields, J. (1972) *Schizophrenia and Genetics: A Twin Study Vantage Point*. Academic Press, London and New York.

Gould, A. (1995) Young carers in Sweden. In *Young Carers in Europe: An Exploratory Cross-National Study in Britain, France, Sweden and Germany* (Ed by S. Becker), pp. 49–63. Young Carers Research Group in association with the European Research Centre, Loughborough University, Loughborough.

Greater Manchester Black Young Carers Working Group (1996) *Working with Black Young Carers: A Framework for Change*. The Greater Manchester Black Young Carers Working Group, Manchester.

Griffiths, Sir R. (1988) *Community Care: Agenda for Action*. HMSO, London.

Grimshaw, R. (1991) *Children of Parents with Parkinson's Disease: A Research Report for the Parkinson's Disease Society*. National Children's Bureau, London.

Hantrais, L. (1992a) La fécondité en France et au Royaume-Uni et les effets possibles de la politique familiale. *Population*, 47, 4, 987–1016.

Hantrais, L. (1992b) Les systèmes d'aide et de protection sociale à l'épreuve des structures familiales. Le cas du Royaume-Uni. *Recherche Sociale*, 122, Avril–Juin, *Les Failles de la Protection Sociale en Europe*, 113–29.

Hantrais, L. (1994) Comparing family policy in Britain, France and Germany. *Journal of Social Policy*, 23, 2, 135–60.

Hantrais, L. (1995) *Social Policy in the European Union*. Macmillan, London.

Hantrais, L. & Becker, S. (1995) Young carers in Europe: a comparative perspective. In *Young Carers in Europe: An Exploratory Cross-National Study in Britain, France, Sweden and Germany* (Ed by S. Becker), pp. 77–92. Young Carers Research Group in association with the European Research Centre, Loughborough University, Loughborough.

Hardiker, P., Exton, K. & Barker, M. (1991) The social policy contexts of prevention in child care. *British Journal of Social Work*, 21, 341–59.

Hatfield, A.B. (1978) Psychological costs of schizophrenia to the family. *Social Work*, 23, 5, 355–9.

Hearn, B. (1997) Putting support and protection into practice. In *Child Protection and Family Support: Tensions, Contradictions and Possibilities* (Ed by N. Parton), pp. 223–41. Routledge, London.

Hendessi, M. (1996) *Report of the Survey of Young Carers in Hammersmith and Fulham*. Caring for Carers Association, London.

Heslinga, K., Schellen, A. & Verkuyl, A. (1974) *Not Made of Stone: The Sexual Problems of Handicapped People*. Charles C. Thomas, Springfield, Illinois.

Hilbourne, J. (1973) On disabling the normal. *British Journal of Social Work*, 2, 4, 497–507.

HMSO (1969) *Report of the Committee of Inquiry into Allegations of Ill-Treatment of Patients and other Irregularities at the Ely Hospital, Cardiff.* Cmnd 3975, HMSO, London.

HMSO (1990) *Community Care in the Next Decade and Beyond.* HMSO, London.

HMSO (1994) *The UK's First Report to the UN Committee on the Rights of the Child.* HMSO, London.

Hugman, R. (1994) *Ageing and the Care of Older People in Europe.* Macmillan, London.

Imrie, J. & Coombes, Y. (1995) *No Time to Waste: The Scale and Dimensions of the Problem of Children Affected by HIV/AIDS in the United Kingdom.* Barnardo's, Ilford.

James, A. & Prout, A. (Eds) (1990) *Constructing and Reconstructing Childhood.* Falmer Press, Basingstoke.

James, A. & Prout, A. (1996) Strategies and structures: towards a new perspective on children's experiences of family life. In *Children in Families: Research and Policy* (Ed by J. Brannen & M. O'Brien), pp. 41–52. Falmer Press, London.

James, A. & Prout, A. (Eds) (1997) *Constructing and Reconstructing Childhood,* 2nd edn. Falmer Press, Basingstoke.

Jani-Le Bris, H. (1993) *Family Care of Dependent Older People in the European Community.* European Foundation for the Improvement of Living and Working Conditions, Dublin.

Joshi, H. (1992) The cost of caring. In *Women and Poverty in Britain: the 1990s* (Ed by C. Glendinning & J. Millar), pp. 110–25. Harvester Wheatsheaf, Hemel Hempstead.

Kamerman, S.B. & Kahn, A.K. (1978) *Family Policy: Government and Families in Fourteen Countries.* Columbia University Press, New York.

Keith, L. & Morris, J. (1995) Easy targets: a disability rights perspective on the 'children as carers' debate. *Critical Social Policy,* 44/45, 36–57.

Kossoris, P. (1970) Family therapy. *American Journal of Nursing,* 70, 1730–3.

Krulik, T., Katz, S., Hayout, I., Florian, V. & Gorani, N. (1997) *Research Proposal – Children of Chronically Ill Mothers: The Relationship between the Child's Involvement in the Care of the Mother, and Social Behaviour.* Department of Nursing, Tel Aviv University, mimeo.

Laing, R.D. (1959) *The Divided Self.* Penguin, Harmondsworth.

Land, H. (1987) Who cares for the family? *Journal of Social Policy,* 7, 3, 257–84.

Landells, S. & Pritlove, J. (1994) *Young Carers of a Parent with Schizophrenia: A Leeds Survey.* Leeds City Council, Department of Social Services, Leeds.

Laroque, M-F. (1985) La protection sociale des personnes âgées. *Revue Française des Affaires Sociales,* 39, July–September, 179–95.

Lefranc, C. (1994) Households and families in France, Germany and Great Britain: statistical constructions and national realities. *Cross-National Research Papers,* 4, 1, 17–33.

Lenoir, R. (1991) Politique familiale et construction sociale de la famille. *Revue Françiase de Science Politique,* 41, 6, 781–807.

Lewis, F.M., Ellison, E.S. & Woods, N.F. (1985) The impact of breast cancer on the family. *Seminars in Oncology Nursing,* 1, 3, 206–13.

Lewis, J. & Meredith, B. (1988) *Daughters Who Care: Daughters Caring for Mothers at Home.* Routledge, London.

Lidz, T. & Fleck, S. (1965) *Schizophrenia and the Family*. International Universities Press, New York.

Lister, R. & Becker, S. (1994) Care and the community. In *Focus on Britain: Review of 1993* (Ed by P. Allan, J. Benyon & B. McCormick), pp. 180–4. Perennial Publications, Oxford.

Lloyd, E. (1997) The role of the centre in family support. In *Social Action with Children and Families: A Community Development Approach to Child and Family Welfare* (Ed by C. Cannan & C. Warren), pp. 143–61. Routledge, London.

Lunn, T. (1990) A new awareness. *Community Care* ('Inside' supplement), February 22, viii.

Lynch, E.W. & Bakley, S. (1989) Serving young children whose parents are mentally retarded. *Infants and Young Children*, 1, 3, 26–38.

MacDonald, G. & Roberts, H. (1995) *What Works in the Early Years?* Barnardo's, Ilford.

Mahon, A. & Higgins, J. (1995) '... *A Life of our Own' Young Carers: An Evaluation of Three RHA Funded Projects in Merseyside*. University of Manchester, Health Services Management Unit, Manchester.

Marsden, R. (1995) *Young Carers and Education*. London Borough of Enfield, Education Department, London.

Marsh, P. & Crow, G. (1997) *Family Group Conferences in Child Welfare*. Blackwell Science, Oxford.

Martin, J.P. (1984) *Hospitals in Trouble*. Blackwell, Oxford.

Martin, J. & White, A. (1988) *The Financial Circumstances of Disabled Adults Living in Private Households*. OPCS/HMSO, London.

McLaughlin, M.M. (1974) Survivers and surrogates. In *The History of Childhood* (Ed by L. De Mause), pp. 101–82. Souvenir Press, London and New York.

Mednick, S.A., Mura, E., Schulsinger, F. & Mednick, B. (1982) Perinatal conditions and infant development in children with schizophrenic parents. *Social Biology*, 29, 3–4, 264–75.

Meredith, H. (1991a) Young carers: the unacceptable face of community care. *Social Work and Social Sciences Review*, 3 (supplement), 47–51.

Meredith, H. (1991b) Young carers. *Contact*, summer, 14–15.

Meredith, H. (1992) Supporting the young carer. *Community Outlook*, 2, 5, 15–18.

Meulders-Klein, M-T. & Théry, I. (1993) *Les recompositions familiales aujourd'hui*. Nathan, Coll, Essais & Recherches, Paris.

Millar, J. & Warman, A. (1996) *Family Obligations in Europe*. Family Policy Studies Centre, London.

Monnier, A. & Guibert-Lantoine, C. de (1993) La conjoncture démographique: l'Europe et les pays développés d'Outre Mer. *Population*, 48, 4, 1043–67.

Morris, J. (1991) *Pride Against Prejudice*. Women's Press, London.

Morris, J. (1993) *Independent Lives*. Macmillan, Basingstoke.

Morris, J. (1995) Easy targets: a disability rights perspective on the 'young carers' debate. In *Young Carers: Something to Think About. Papers presented at four SSI workshops May–July 1995*, pp. 38–62. Department of Health, London.

Morris, J. (1997) A response to Aldridge and Becker – disability rights and the denial of young carers: the dangers of zero-sum arguments. *Critical Social Policy*, 17, 133–5.

Morris, P. (1969) *Put Away*. Routledge and Kegan Paul, London.

Munday, B. & Ely, P. (Eds) (1996) *Social Care in Europe*. Prentice Hall, London.

National Health Service and Community Care Act 1990. HMSO, London.

Newell, P. (1991) *The UN Convention and Children's Rights in the UK*. NCB, London.

Newman, T. (1996) Rights, rites and responsibilities: the age of transition to the adult world. In *Young People's Social Attitudes: Having Their Say: The Views of 12–19 Year Olds* (Ed by H. Roberts & D. Sachdev), pp. 6–22. Barnardo's, Ilford.

Newton, B. & Becker, S. (1996) *Young Carers in Southwark: The Hidden Face of Community Care*. Young Carers Research Group, Loughborough University, Loughborough.

Nissel, M. & Bonnerjea, L. (1982) *Family Care of the Handicapped Elderly: Who Pays?* Policy Studies Institute, London.

Nocon, A. & Qureshi, H. (1996) *Outcomes of Community Care for Users and Carers: A Social Services Perspective*. Open University Press, Buckingham.

Nolan, M., Grant, G. & Keady, J. (1996) *Understanding Family Care: A Multidimensional Model of Caring and Coping*. Open University Press, Buckingham.

Office for National Statistics (ONS) (1996) *Young Carers and their Families*. The Stationery Office, London.

Office of Population Censuses and Surveys (OPCS) (1992) *General Household Survey: Carers in 1990*. OPCS Monitor, SS 92/2. HMSO, London.

Olgas, M. (1974) The relationship between parents' health status and body image of their children. *Nursing Research*, 23, 4, 319–24.

Oliver, M. (1989) Disability and dependency: a creation of industrial societies. In *Disability and Dependency* (Ed by L. Barton), pp. 50–60. Falmer Press, London.

Oliver, M. (1990) *The Politics of Disablement*. Macmillan, London.

Olsen, E. (1970) The impact of serious illness on the family system. *Postgraduate Medicine*, 47, 169–74.

Olsen, R. (1996) Young carers: challenging the facts and politics of research into children and caring. *Disability and Society*, 11, 1, 41–54.

O'Brien, J. and Tyne, A. (1981) *The Principle of Normalisation: A Foundation for Effective Services*. Values Into Action, London.

O'Neill, A. (1988) *Young Carers: The Tameside Research*. Tameside Metropolitan Borough Council, Tameside.

O'Neill, A.M. (1985) Normal and bright children of mentally retarded parents: the Huck Finn syndrome. *Child Psychiatry and Human Development*, 15, 4, 255–68.

Orvaschel, H., Weissman, M.M. & Kidd K.K. (1980) Children and depression. *Journal of Affective Disorders*, 2, 1–16.

Page, R. (1988) *Report on the Initial Survey Investigating the Number of Young Carers in Sandwell Secondary Schools*. Sandwell Metropolitan Borough Council, Sandwell.

Parker, G. (1992) Counting care: numbers and types of informal carers. In *Carers: Research and Practice* (Ed by J. Twigg), pp. 6–29. HMSO, London.

Parker, G. (1994) *Where Next for Research on Carers?* Nuffield Community Care Studies Centre, University of Leicester, Leicester.

Parker, G. & Olsen, R. (1995) A sideways glance at young carers. In *Young Carers: Something to Think About. Papers presented at four SSI workshops May–July 1995*, pp. 63–74. Department of Health, London.

Parton, N. (1997) Child protection and family support: current debates and future prospects. In *Child Protection and Family Support: Tensions, Contradictions and Possibilities* (Ed by N. Parton), pp. 1–24. Routledge, London.

Pauti, A. (1992) La politique familiale en Suède. *Population*, 47, 4, 961–85.

Pederson, L.M. & Valanis, B.G. (1988) The effects of breast cancer on the family: a review of the literature. *Journal of Psychosocial Oncology*, 6, 1–2, 95–118.

Powell, M. & Kocher, P. (1996) *Strategies for Change: A Carers Impact Resource Book*. King's Fund Publishing, London.

Power, P.W. (1977) The adolescent's reaction to chronic illness of a parent: some implications for family counseling. *International Journal of Family Counseling*, 5, 70–8.

Price, K. (1996) *How do I Get them to Come? Interim Report*. Interchange Respite Care (NSW) Incorporated, Waverley, Australia.

Qvortrup, J. (1996) Foreword. In *Children and Families: Research and Policy* (Ed by J. Brannen & M. O'Brien), pp. xi–xiii. Falmer Press, London.

Ramon, S. (1987) The making of a professional culture: professionals in psychiatry in Britain and Italy since 1945. *Cross-National Research Papers*, 1, 3, 35–49.

Raymond, M., Slaby, A. & Lieb, J. (1975) *The Healing Alliance*. W.W. Norton & Co., New York.

Rieder, R.O. (1973) The offspring of schizophrenic parents: a review. *Journal of Nervous and Mental Disease*, 157, 3, 179–90.

Roberts, H. & Sachdev, D. (Eds) (1996) *Young People's Social Attitudes: Having Their Say: The Views of 12–19 Year Olds*. Barnardo's, Ilford.

Romano, M.D. (1976) Preparing children for parental disability. *Social Work in Health Care*, 1, 3, 309–15.

Rosenberg, S.A. & McTate, G.A. (1982) Intellectually handicapped mothers: problems and prospects. *Children Today*, 11, 1, 24–6.

Ruxton, S. (1996) *Children in Europe*. NCH Action for Children, London.

Sargent, K.L. (1985) Helping children cope with parental mental illness through use of children's literature. *Child Welfare*, 64, 6, 617–28.

Scelles, R. (1994) L'incidence psychologique sur les frères et soeurs de la présence d'un enfant handicapé dans la famille. *Dialogue – Recherches Cliniques et Sociologiques sur le Couple et la Famille*, 2ème trimestre, 79–89.

Schaff, C. (1993) From dependency to self advocacy: redefining disability. *The American Journal of Occupational Therapy*, 47, 10, 943–8.

Schiff, N.B. & Ventry, I.M. (1976) Communication problems in hearing children of deaf parents. *Journal of Speech and Hearing Disorders*, 41, 348–58.

Schilling, R.F., Schinke, S.P., Blythe, B.J. & Barth, R.P. (1982) Child maltreatment and mentally retarded parents: is there a relationship? *Mental Retardation*, 20, 5, 201–9.

Schultheis, F. (1990) Familles d'Europe sans frontières: un enjeu social par dessus le marché. *Actes du Colloque Familles d'Europe sans Frontières*, 4–5 December, 1989, 73–80.

Schultheis, F. (1991) La famille, le marché et l'état providence. In *Affaires de Famille, Affaires d'État* (Ed by F. Singly & F. Schultheis), pp. 33–42. Jarville la Magrange, Éditions de l'Est.

Schultheis, F. (1992) Inerties structurelles et ambivalences idéologiques: la protection sociale allemande face aux nouveaux 'risques familiaux'. *Recherche Sociale*, 122, April–June, *Les Failles de la Protection Sociale en Europe*, 144–57.

Schumacher, K.L. (1995) Family caregiver role acquisition: role-making through situated interaction. *Scholarly Inquiry for Nursing Practice: An International Journal*, 9, 3, 211–26.

Schur, E.M. (1971) *Labelling Deviant Behaviour: Its Sociological Implications*. Harper and Row, New York.

The Scottish Office (1996) *Community Care in Scotland: Carers (Recognition and Services) Act 1995. Policy and Practice Guidance*. The Scottish Office, Social Work Services Group, Circular no. SWSG11/96, Edinburgh.

Seagull, E.A. & Scheurer, S.L. (1986) Neglected and abused children of mentally retarded parents. *Child Abuse and Neglect*, 10, 493–500.

Segal, J. & Simkins, J. (1993) *My Mum Needs Me: Helping Children with Ill or Disabled Parents*. Penguin, Harmondsworth.

Segal, J. & Simkins, J. (1996) *Helping Children with Ill or Disabled Parents: A Guide for Parents and Professionals*. Jessica Kingsley, London.

Seifer, R., Sameroff, A.J. & Jones, F. (1981) Adaptive behaviour in young children of emotionally disturbed women. *Journal of Applied Developmental Psychology*, 1, 4, 251–76.

Social Services Inspectorate (1995) Letter to all Directors of Social Services, 28 April.

Sturges, J.S. (1977) Talking with children about mental illness in the family. *Health and Social Work*, 2, 3, 88–109.

Sturges, J.S. (1978) Children's reactions to mental illness in the family. *Social Casework*, 59, 9, 530–6.

Sundel, M. & Homan, C.C. (1979) Prevention in child welfare: a framework for management and practice. *Child Welfare*, 58, 510–21.

Swain, J., Finklestein, V., French, S. & Oliver, M. (1993) *Disabling Barriers, Enabling Environments*. Open University Press, Buckingham.

Szasz, T. (1972) *The Myth of Mental Illness*. Granada Publishing Ltd, London.

Thompson, A. (1997) Where to now? *Community Care*, 6–12 March, 20–21.

Thompson, P., Lavery, J. & Curtice, J. (1990) *Short Changed by Disability*. Disablement Income Group, London.

Torkelson, R., Lynch, R. & Thomas, K. (1994) People with disabilities as victims: changing an ill-advised paradigm. *Journal of Rehabilitation*, March, 8–15.

Towell, D. (Ed.) (1988) *An Ordinary Life in Practice*. King Edward Hospital Fund for London, London.

Townsend, P. (1962) *The Last Refuge: A Survey of Residential Institutions and Homes for the Aged in England and Wales*. Routledge and Kegan Paul, London.

Trenery, D. (unpublished) *Coordination, Implementation and Community Care*. MA thesis, Loughborough University.

Tunnard, J. (1997) Mechanisms for empowerment: family group conferences and local family advocacy schemes. In *Social Action with Children and*

Families: A Community Development Approach to Child and Family Welfare (Ed by C. Cannan & C. Warren), pp. 162–81. Routledge, London.

Tunstill, J. (1997) Implementing the family support clauses of the 1989 Children Act. In *Child Protection and Family Support: Tensions, Contradictions and Possibilities* (Ed by N. Parton), pp. 39–58. Routledge, London.

Twigg, J., Atkin, K. & Perring, C. (1990) *Carers and Services: A Review of Research*. HMSO, London.

Tyler, A. (1990) Helping the children to cope.... *Combat*, 37, 16–20.

Ungerson, C. (1987) *Policy is Personal: Sex, Gender and Informal Care*. Tavistock, London.

Ungerson, C. (Ed.) (1990) *Gender and Caring: Work and Welfare in Britain and Scandinavia*. Harvester Wheatsheaf, London.

Walmsley, J. (1993) Contradictions in caring: reciprocity and interdependence. *Disability, Handicap and Society*, 8, 2, 129–41.

Warner, N. (1994) *Community Care: Just a Fairy Tale?* Carers National Association, London.

Warner, N. (1995) *Better Tomorrows: Report of a National Study of Carers and the Community Care Changes*. Carers National Association, London.

Warren, C. (1997) Family support and the journey to empowerment. In *Social Action with Children and Families: A Community Development Approach to Child and Family Welfare* (Ed by C. Cannan & C. Warren), pp. 103–23. Routledge, London.

Weitz, D. (1994) Everybody must get stoned. *Changes: An International Journal of Psychology and Psychotherapy*, 12, 1, 50–59.

West, M.L. & Keller, A.E.R. (1991) Parentification of the child: a case study of Bowlby's compulsive care-giving attachment pattern. *American Journal of Psychotherapy*, 45, 3, 425–31.

White, P. (1989) Caring for the caring. *Young People Now*, June, 23.

Wolfensberger, W. (1972) *The Principle of Normalisation in Human Services*. National Institute on Mental Retardation, Toronto.

Woods, N.F., Yates, B.C. & Primomo, J. (1989) Supporting families during chronic illness. *IMAGE: Journal of Nursing Scholarship*, 21, 1, 46–50.

World Health Organisation (1982) *Manuals on Child Mental Health and Psychosocial Development*. WHO, Geneva.

Index